Los

WHY I LOVE AND LEFT
MY MORMON FAITH

HULA INK
www.hulaink.com

In cooperation with Astrid Ule

ISBN-13: 978-3-946213-12-3

An original edition
by Hula Ink
an Eric T. Hansen Publisher
Berlin, Germany

Edited by Astrid Ule
Cover design by Andreas Rupprecht, Berlin
Layout by John L. Grantham, Potsdam

www.hulaink.de

For A.,

and for John Willenberg,

and for the ward in Munich,
which I left without a word of explanation.
I'm making up for that now.

Losing My Religion

WHY I LOVE AND LEFT
MY MORMON FAITH

by Eric T. Hansen

Contents

FOREWORD

The Black Pit

I MET DEATH FOR THE FIRST TIME IN KREFELD.

Krefeld is a beautiful, clean little German town between the Rhine and the Dutch border. I had come here on a two-year mission for the Mormon church, in which I was raised and in which I believed. My job was to knock on doors and hand out pamphlets to strangers in an attempt to get them interested in the faith I loved so much that I was willing to sacrifice two years of my life in a foreign country to share it with the world. It was the early eighties, I was nineteen and this was the first time I had been away from home for an extended period.

The man who taught me about death seemed like a nice guy at first. Young, thin, well groomed, intelligent, probing eyes. We met on the street. My missionary companion and I offered him a pamphlet about the church and we talked a while. He said he wanted to hear more. He invited us to come to his apartment a week later. He said he wanted to read up a little first.

When we arrived, he was prepared. He sat us down on his couch and started talking. We had expected to do the talking. He had spent the week reading up on everything he could find about the Mormons, and for two hours he explained to us in excruciating detail everything that was wrong with Mormonism.

He started with Joseph Smith, the 19th century church founder, and his many sins, mainly his multiple wives, some of whom were underage when he used his authority as self-proclaimed "prophet" to pressure them into marrying him; some were already wives of other men at the time. He went on to the bloody Mountain Meadows Massacre, in which Mormons slaughtered over a hundred unarmed men, women and children. He explained why the Book of Mormon was a fraud, how the rites of the Mormon temple were stolen from the Freemasons, and more. Much more.

For the first half hour or so, I took it. When you believe in something like I believed in the church, you can accept a lot of contradictions without wincing. Think of the Catholics and the virgin birth. Catholics aren't dumb. They know there is no such thing, but it doesn't contradict their faith because faith stands above mundane biology.

For me, it was the theory of evolution. I was raised to take science seriously. It was never questioned in our household. For many people, evolution contradicts God, for us it didn't. On the contrary, we often speculated on how God must have used evolution to create life on earth. Surely, God too has to utilize the laws of nature to do what he does. It was easy for me to get past the theory of evolution and still believe.

It should have been easy for me to get past what this man was telling us, too. Okay, Joseph Smith lied about having more than one wife. So what? Mormons killed innocent civilians in the heat and confusion of the mid-19th century Mormon Wars. Do you know how many deaths the Catholic Church directly and indirectly caused in its history? These are horrible things, but they don't disprove faith.

What I couldn't get past was the sheer volume of his arguments. And this man presented them in bulk. It was endless. He made the church seem like it was invented by the Devil himself. After an hour or so of fighting off his attack, we just sat there, dumbfounded, and took the battering he gave us. Nothing in the world was as bad as the Mormons. By comparison, the witch hunts, the Inquisition and the Crusades were almost positive. After all, the Inquisition and the Crusades had ended, but the perpetration of the delusions upon millions of people all over the world by the Mormon church continues to this day.

The blast of hatred was too strong; the doubts he awoke in us came too fast and were too many for us to beat back. In the end, he was victorious.

I remember shaking his hand, thanking him politely for the pleasant talk, assuring him that there are answers to all the questions he posed, walking out of that apartment, down the street and crossing a large parking lot behind the open-roofed shopping mall the Germans call a *Fußgängerzone*, or "pedestrian zone."

That's when it hit me. I had to stop. I felt weak. For the first time in my life I seriously considered the idea that the church might be a fraud: If even half – no, if even a third of his claims were true, how could I stay in this church? But it was even more than that: If this church was not true in all it pretended to be, then no church was true, no religion was true, and ultimately God did not exist.

I understood the final consequence immediately: If my faith was a lie, then death was not a step into a new stage of life, but a step into nothingness.

In that moment the parking lot seemed to open up beneath me into a bottomless pit, and I saw what I had never seen before: Without the church, without God, without faith, death is an endless black hole from which nothing can escape, not life, not love, not humanity, not meaning. And certainly not I.

I have never felt so alone, before or since. I have never felt so vulnerable. I have never been so overwhelmed by raw meaninglessness. The sun seemed to turn black in the sky, it felt like I was walking home in darkness in the middle of the day.

I never did recover, not fully.

In a few days I got back to the point where I could function. I was eventually able to recognize that the young man had wanted to hurt us. He simply loved destroying things that were important to other people. There is a part of our culture that celebrates what Germans call *Rechthaberei* – being right. If you can prove someone else wrong, you are superior. That's all he was doing.

But I had already seen the black pit. I could not unsee it. That vision would never go away. I still see it today.

I didn't know it then, but that was the beginning of the end of my faith.

I count three great prayers in my life: Three major prayers I still think about today, three prayers that shaped who I am.

My first great prayer took place when I was eight, my last when I was thirty. In the first two, I expected an answer from God and received one. In the last prayer, I did not.

I remember that first prayer well.

It was in Hawaii, where I had moved with my parents and five brothers and sisters two years before. We were Mormons all. It was normal for me to go to church every Sunday, I had never thought twice about it, but the closer my eighth birthday approached, the more I realized that baptism was a serious decision.

Mormons don't baptize infants. Children are baptized at eight, earliest. Again and again my parents and my Sunday school teacher made it clear to me that I would soon be expected to decide whether to get baptized or not. They stressed that it was my decision and mine alone. Especially my father made sure I understood that.

I didn't know what to do. I thought about it day and night. There must have been a right answer, but there was no one there to give it to me. For the first time in my life, I was left alone with a major decision. That doesn't often happen to an eight-year old.

So I did what all Mormons do when they face an important decision they cannot make alone: I prayed.

On several nights, one after the other, alone in my room, I kneeled at my bedside and asked God if the church was true.

When Mormons talk about the church being "true," they are saying a lot: that God himself created the church and leads it today, that he accepts no other church, that he appeared to Joseph Smith and gave him the "golden plates;" that he speaks to the prophets – the leaders of the church – and more. All that is embodied in the typically Mormon sentence, "I know the church is true."

But they don't arrive at that conviction by arguing the pros and cons of Mormonism. They get there by putting the question to God in prayer, and by expecting God to answer. I wasn't asking God whether I should join the church or not – that was not the question. I wanted to know if it was true. If it was, I had no choice but to be baptized. If not, I was free to do as I wished.

After two or three nights of feeling vaguely silly, I knew the only way I would get an answer was to force God to give me one. That night I stayed on my knees until the answer came.

It took a while. Probably not an hour, but close. At some point I noticed something. It was just there, as if it had always been there, but I'd only just now noticed it: a warm glow. My heart beat faster. At first I wondered: Is this God talking to me? Then that melodrama faded and was replaced with a firm confidence. It was a feeling, much like love is a feeling. It's just there, deep inside you, you can't do anything about it. I had no choice: I believed that the church was true whether I liked it or not.

I didn't tell my parents. They didn't ask.

Next Sunday after services I had an appointment with the bishop – the head of our little "ward" or congregation in Kailua, where we lived, a nice family father everyone liked. He asked me to step into his office. I sat before his desk while my parents waited outside. He explained to me what baptism meant: I would be entering into a commitment with God, a "covenant" to honor him and his son Jesus Christ, to serve and obey him, to always behave in life in a way that would please God. He explained that when I die and stand before God, he would expect more of me than of others who did not enter into this covenant. He made me understand the decision I faced now was nothing less than how I would lead my entire future life.

Then he asked if I wanted to be baptized. I said, "Yes."

He congratulated me, we shook hands, and I stepped out of his office and into the nearly empty parking lot where my parents and my brothers and sisters were waiting in the car, and I told them my decision.

"Good," said my father. "Now let's go have lunch."

The baptism itself wasn't in Kailua, but in the "stake center," the central church building responsible for the administration of the various other wards on the island. Early Sunday morning our parents loaded us into our best clothes and then into the station wagon, and we drove over the Pali ridge that cut the island of Oahu in half and on to Honolulu on the other side.

I can't say what the little suit I wore looked like, I only know it was scratchy and stiff. I know I had short hair – a crew cut, as my father cut the boys hair himself, and he worked for the army.

After the church meetings, my father led me down some stairs into a basement I hadn't known was there before and into a locker room, where we dressed in white. Then we entered a small room with a low ceiling where my mother and my brothers and sisters and a few others waited on folding chairs.

In the middle of the room a large, round basin was set into the floor. My father and I walked down the steps into the lukewarm water. It came up to my waist. He positioned me a little toward the front and stood beside me. He raised his right hand above his head as in a vow and spoke a prayer that ended with the words, "I baptize you in the name of the Father, the Son and the Holy Ghost."

Then he said, "Hold your nose and bend your knees." He laid one hand on the small of my back and with the other on my chest, he pushed me down into the water – all the way under, not a single hair was allowed to float above the surface, otherwise we'd have to repeat the process. After a worryingly long moment, he pulled me back up a baptized member of the Church of Jesus Christ of Latter-Day Saints.

I saw no light shining down from heaven. I heard no voices. My heart was not suddenly filled with joy. My thoughts during the baptism were mostly practical – I worried that my feet might slip out from under me and float above the surface – I'd been warned about that – or that I couldn't hold my breath long enough. Nervous. During the baptism I was mainly nervous.

What's burned into my memory is the ride back home from Honolulu.

My little sister and I sat in the very back of the station wagon, our knees up to our chins. I was quiet. I was thinking.

I had just made the most important decision of my life. I'm sure the bishop, in our little talk together, had even used that phrase, "the most important decision of your life." I was aware of my entire future stretching out before me like a road. I had just chosen which road I was going to take. It was my own decision, it was my road. No one's but mine. Suddenly, I could see all along it right up to the end.

When I tell non-Mormons today about my baptism, they act vaguely irritated. "A kid that young is not old enough to make independent decisions," they say.

They are not entirely wrong, of course. If you get baptized in the faith of your parents when you are eight, you might imagine you're making your own decision, but a large part of it is simply fulfilling the expectations of Mom and Dad. I thought long and hard about taking this step, but my parents knew all along what I was going to do.

But I didn't know.

For me, it was an independent decision. And it changed the way I looked at my life. From then on, my life was mine.

If you grow up outside a church, you most likely make your first significant decision after puberty, when you decide on a profession or whether to go to college or not. Mormon children make their first life-changing decision at eight. They learn that early that the responsibility for their lives lies wholly in their own hands. When I think about Mormonism, the good and the bad, this is one of the things I admire.

Some say that the idea of the individual is a modern invention. Some even say that the individual as we think of it today is an American invention. What is certainly true is that the idea of the individual has a special place in the American mentality – the individual as captain of his fate, the self-reliant human being responsible for himself and possessing the God-given right to his life according to his own will. For Mormons, this deeply American conviction is not just a vague concept, it is anchored in the theology, and Mormon kids internalize the idea from the very beginning.

On that drive back from Honolulu, as I sat in the back with my little sister and thought about my life spreading out before me, I smiled.

When ex-Mormons write about their experiences with the church, it often ends up a bitter reckoning: How the church lied to them, how it manipulates its members and makes them believe in crazy fairy-tales any reasonable person would immediately recognize as nonsense. I understand the bitterness. If you grow up in the church and leave it as an adult, as I did, you often have the feeling that it robbed you of half your life. And in some cases, the church can do real damage.

But most of the time I am reminded of the man or woman fresh off a divorce who says, “It was the worst mistake of my life – I can’t believe I stayed ten years in that marriage.” But if you remained ten years with him or her, there must have been something more to that relationship than you are telling us.

I lost my faith over twenty years ago, and in that time the Mormon church has not faded into a distant memory. On the contrary, it has come more into focus for me, until now I believe I see it clearly – in all its glory and its shame. I am overwhelmed by some of the things I see. When I look at the Mormon church, I see the most intelligent, the most modern and the most radical Christian church I know. It is also the most American church – perhaps the only truly American church. No other religion has the daring to propose a heaven where every man can still pursue his dreams. The radicalism of the American Dream is deeply embedded in Mormonism. That’s what I love about this church even today, though I love it from a distance.

Then there’s the story of how I lost my faith – why I left the church and can never return.

People who have never believed often don’t understand what it means to lose your faith. It’s more than just quitting a club. The church accompanied me through most of my life; it was intimately involved in my thinking, my decisions, my moral judgment, my growth, in who I am. It was more than an institution; it was a part of me.

Nonbelievers tend to imagine losing your religion in terms of having more time on your hands Sunday mornings, or of not liking the pastor and his sermons, or that you finally realized how stupid this whole religion thing was and have become an atheist. And because Mormons don’t drink alcohol or engage in premarital sex, you also get a few jabs in the ribs, as if finally you can go out and have a good time.

But it's more than that. Without God, there is no meaning to life. That's what gets taken from you. Before losing your religion, death is not very scary. When God suddenly disappears out of your life, death becomes absolute and you realize no matter what you do in life, it is pointless, for it will all disappear in a few years anyway, as if it had never happened. That's the horror of losing your religion.

When I lost my faith, a vast sense of loss descended upon me and I recognized that a part of my soul had been wrenched out of me, leaving only the second-best parts, the ragged and crippled rest, and that everything good and beautiful about this life on earth – God watching over us, the promise that we will return to him, the closeness to him, the vibrancy and clarity and hope he provided, the promise that the end of this life was only the beginning of another – that was gone and replaced with nothing – no hope, no love, no purpose.

Without faith, I had no reason to live. So I had to find one.

CHAPTER 1

A Boy With the Big Idea

WHENEVER I READ IN THE PAPERS THAT SOME crazy guy somewhere has once again spoken with God and knows that the world is going to end next week, I roll my eyes a little and turn the page. Maybe I make fun of him when I next have a beer with friends if there's nothing more entertaining to talk about. Never in my life have I felt the need to go out and kill him.

We are surprisingly quick to talk about committing murder – "I could just kill that guy!" But psychologists say killing someone requires an almost superhuman emotional commitment. That's why it happens so seldom. Even people who hate each other to the core very rarely murder each other. And for an average guy to leave his house and family one night with a gun and kill a complete stranger just because he has differing religious or political opinions is so rare as to be almost impossible. Look at the list of assassinations of political or religious leaders from Lincoln to Martin Luther King – compared to the sheer number of political and religious leaders in the world, that list is astoundingly short and generally reserved for high-profile names. Your local pastor will probably never make the list, nor will the guy who thinks the world is going to end Tuesday. None of the founders of such controversial religious communities like Christian Science, the Jehovah's Witnesses, the Seventh-day Adventists or Scientology were ever murdered.

Why then did Joseph Smith, of all people, have to die?

In the early 19th century, the Wild West was not actually out west – it began in the western half of New York State.

The railroad had yet to be invented. The US only had 22 states and New York State, which bordered on Canada to the north and the Great Lakes to the west, was sparsely populated. For a lot of farmers out there, the distance to the next shop was a day's ride. Many didn't see a larger city their entire lives. Life was lonely and hard, there was no social security or police nearby. The nights were darker than most of us today can imagine and the opportunities to make your fortune were severely limited.

For many people, faith was the only light at the end of the tunnel.

Beginning in the South, a religious fever called the Second Great Awakening consumed the continent. Suddenly, everyone had a personal relationship with Jesus. The established Protestant churches – especially the Baptists and Methodists – expanded swiftly and new sects popped up everywhere. A similar phenomenon was underway in Europe, and it inspired waves of emigration to the States, further swelling American churches.

It was a heyday for itinerant preachers. Churches were often few and far between, so the revivalists traveled from village to village, setting up tents and attracting audiences from far and wide before moving on. On the well-trodden paths between east and west and leading from the south to Canada and back, evangelists crossed and re-crossed one region more than most others: western New York State. The area saw so many wandering preachers that it received the nickname "burned-over district."

And it wasn't just revivalists. Snake-oil salesmen, soothsayers and other charlatans took the same routes, hawking their exotic and exciting new products, making big promises, and the people, driven to superstition by dark, lonely nights, accepted every new thing no matter how bizarre. Their love of faith on the one hand and superstition on the other were so strong that they did not always differentiate between the two.

In this burned-over district, Joseph Smith grew up, born in 1805, when the nation was not quite 30 years old, among farmers, immigrants, revivalists, quacks and magic. It became evident early on that his ambitions – and he was clearly ambitious – did not tend toward farming. The only question was whether he would become a con man or a preacher.

A popular scam in the region combined superstition with the *ur*-American pursuit of wealth: Treasure hunters claiming they could, with the help of a divining rod or a magic stone or some similar device, find hidden treasure. (We laugh at this foolishness and shake our heads today, but belief in things like magic stones is still alive and well: A few streets from where I live in Berlin, a successful shop sells "healing" stones of all colors and shapes.)

Early on, Smith found work as a treasure hunter for hire, usually working in teams and often using a "seer stone." Professional treasure hunters didn't work for themselves, but for clients – that way, if they came up empty-handed, they could still bill their employers. At least once, Smith nabbed a lucrative treasure-hunting commission from a wealthy farmer who, when no riches materialized, took him and his partners to court.

The question comes up again and again if Smith was a fraud, both in his treasure-hunting days and as a prophet, intentionally fooling the people.

When I studied medieval literature in Munich, I read the startlingly beautiful Middle Latin visions of the prophetess Hildegard von Bingen, and I was not the only one to ask whether she really believed God was talking to her, or was she an impostor? Interestingly, our professors were unwilling to just say she was a fake. Instead, they speculated, as we did, that she might have experienced something happening in her mind, maybe even mysterious migraines, which she interpreted as divine. It's hard to know what goes on in anyone's brain. For people like Hildegard and Smith, religion was a very real part of life. Smith's parents searched for religious truth their entire lives and among his relations there were several who claimed to have experienced visions. And it's safe to say that there were very few atheists in the region. There is no evidence that he ever considered himself a fraud, so it's impossible to know whether he believed in his own claims or not.

Back when I was a church member, that question bothered me, for if he lied about the seer stone to defraud wealthy farmers, then he lied about the visions that would come later. Now that I have left the church and no longer have to justify my faith, I see the story differently – not as a question of true or untrue, but as an aspect of his humanity. And I like what I see. I love the idea of this young man out in the middle of nowhere with no future, standing at a crossroads, realizing that he could use his charismatic gift to earn himself a little money treasure hunting now and again, or he could create a religion that, if successful, would change the lives of millions of people.

Mostly, I love the American-ness of his story: That vast primeval chaos of mud, darkness and ignorance boiling over, fusing with desperate superstitions and pseudo-religious fantasies, not to mention a generous pinch of good old American money-grabbing. I love the idea of thousands of mostly immigrant Americans out there in the unpopulated wilderness with nothing to hold onto but their own wild-eyed determination to make something of their lives. I love that vibrant, miserable dogfight that was and is the American dream. And in the middle of all that, something arises: a religion so weird no one can take it seriously, yet so strong no one can ignore it. And this little guy, Joseph, barely educated, no friends in high places, no experience of the outside world, no money to invest, this kid decides to just keep telling his outlandish stories until people notice him.

I imagine that at some point in the life of young Joseph Smith, the moment arrived when he said: "If I want to make a name for myself in this cacophony of religious voices, I need something so big, so different, that no one can compete with it. I need a wholly new direction, a movement that forces you to either hate me or love me – but never lets you ignore me."

Back then, as today, every church, every preacher competed on the market of faith with his own version of Christianity. But you can only compete effectively if the product you offer is different in some way than the others. Thus, one pastor would discover a verse in scripture that forbids the eating of pork and make that his trademark. Someone else would stumble upon a Biblical commandment prohibiting the consumption of blood, and make a big thing out of that. But in the end, these are petty details. Anyone can find some tiny forgotten thing in the scriptures and blow it up into a philosophy. Smith needed something more. That's the only way I can explain what happened.

He was only fourteen, he later claimed, when he wanted to know which of all the contradicting interpretations of the Bible he was hearing was true. He went into the woods to pray and he stayed on his knees until two beings bathed in light appeared above his head: God the Father and his son Jesus Christ. They told him none of the denominations were true; all had fallen away from the true gospel of Christ, but not to worry, God was about to restore the divine truth to earth once more – with the help of Joseph Smith.

The claim – that God rejected all religions on earth – was a killer argument. The weak point of all Christian religions since Martin Luther was that they were based on an interpretation of the Bible, and you can interpret the Bible any way you like. In the end, only God can say if any of these interpretations come close to the truth. Until Joseph Smith, no one had had the guts to just claim: “My interpretation is correct because I got it from God, so there.” When Smith did just that, he robbed every religion of its legitimization.

But he was just getting started. The really big bomb he dropped a few years later:

This time, an angel appeared to him, Moroni by name. Centuries past, this angel had lived as a human in the area and had buried a book in a hill not far from Smith’s home. So it didn’t disintegrate with time, Moroni had engraved his book on golden plates. The book was the work of Moroni’s father, a prophet named Mormon, and contained the writings of many prophets who had lived between 600 before and 400 years after Christ on the American continent – the forefathers of today’s Native Americans. Smith was to dig up the plates and translate them into English with the help of two magical stones called the Urim and Thummim, which would be given him for that purpose.

So that’s what Smith did. In only three months, he wrote “The Book of Mormon.” Then he returned the plates to the angel and they were never seen again. (Early on, the question was asked, “If you expect us to believe your fantastic story, wouldn’t it make sense to hold onto the golden plates?” The official answer is: “God doesn’t want us to know, he wants us to believe.” Nevertheless, Smith is said to have shown the plates to eleven others, who confirmed this on paper.)

The Book of Mormon begins with the tale of a Jewish family at the time of the Biblical prophet Jeremiah. God instructs them to leave Jerusalem and sail into the unknown. Eventually, the family lands somewhere on the South American coast, where the settlers develop a society accompanied by prophets. The Book of Mormon consists of the writings of these prophets over the centuries and tells of the ups and downs of their society depending on whether they followed God’s commandments or not. The climax comes when Jesus Christ visits them. The Bible tells us that Jesus, after he is crucified in Jerusalem and before he rises from the dead, remains in the grave for three days. According to the Book of Mormon, he used these three days to visit his lost sheep in America. There he taught his new gospel of love and repeated much of what he had said in Israel, most famously the Sermon on the Mount.

Mark Twain complained that the Book of Mormon was "printed chloroform" – the miracle of the book, he quipped, was that Joseph Smith was able to stay awake while writing it. And it is true that the book is boring for stretches, but then, so is the Bible. It's also true that some passages mirror Bible passages nearly one-to-one.

It is also a book had a major impact on my life.

When I think of the Book of Mormon, two passages immediately come to mind: one verse I love, another I hate. Here's the one I love:

"For it must needs be, that there is an opposition in all things," written by the prophet Nephi (2. Nephi 2:11).

The principle (which is not new – others, including St. Augustine, wrote about it) is so simple as to be obvious: If you don't know darkness, you can't recognize light; without evil, you cannot see good; no order without chaos, no success without failure, no joy without sorrow, no love without hate. Oh yes, and this: without death, no life.

When I was a kid, I began noticing the strange questions adults sometimes rhetorically – and a little melodramatically – asked, especially "Why do bad things happen to good people?" or, "If there is a God, why does he allow such terrible suffering in this world?" It's because of this verse that I never had the urge to ask those *"Why me?"* questions. Life only makes sense if you experience both extremes. Life without opposites would be monotone, static and pointless. Not only are evil and suffering necessary, but conflict is too. Two people cannot and should not always have the same opinion and goals; endless harmony is not possible and not desirable. It would lead to personal stagnation. We would not grow, we would not change, we would remain blathering, helpless, happy infants all our lives.

With this verse, Nephi taught me the first great paradox of life: that the purpose of life is not happiness or love or success, but life itself, whatever that experience may be. This world with all its wars, diseases, disappointments and conflicts is not imperfect, it is exactly as it should be: That was the intention from the start.

With Nephi's verse in mind, I began appreciating those parts of life I didn't like. If you look closely, ugliness has a certain beauty to it; in ignorance, I sometimes sense a certain kind of wisdom; there are times when loneliness is fulfilling, just as love is, and disappointment can awaken the emotions so violently that you feel your own soul more intensely than before.

I still love that verse.

Then there's the verse I hate more than any other:

"For the natural man is an enemy to God" (Mosiah 3:19).

But more on that later.

When Joseph Smith published the Book of Mormon in 1830 and immediately began baptizing his followers as members of a new church, he was 25 years old. In the same year, the persecution began.

Again and again, Smith had to flee angry mobs or was arrested for public nuisance or on some such trumped-up charge. Eventually it got so bad, the entire fledgling Mormon community fled. That didn't stop the persecution, and once the Mormons got into the habit of fleeing, they had to keep doing it.

They tried rebuilding their religious community in cities in Ohio, Missouri and Illinois, but always, after a few years, they had to pack up and move on. Along the way, Smith mutated from preacher to utopian. In those wild, partly unsettled territories he had converts to organize and feed. He became a banker (didn't work out), mayor (also did not end well), architect (besides the churches, the Mormons built "temples," in which they practiced their most holy rites), urban planner (in Missouri he founded his own city, Nauvoo), even a presidential candidate (needless to say, he lost).

Every time the persecution mounted, Smith fluctuated between fleeing and standing his ground. When he organized his own militia, things only got worse, until the conflict got its own name: In the so-called "Mormon War," Mormons and non-Mormons traded off ambushing, beating and chasing each other and burning down each other's barns. In the "Battle of Crooked River," the Mormons went so far as to attack the state military, which was not smart, and the Governor of Missouri swore to either chase all Mormons out of the state or have them executed. Shortly after that, in the so-called "Haun's Mill massacre," seventeen Mormons were slaughtered.

When the Missouri governor sent in the militia, even Smith knew he didn't have a chance. He surrendered. A military court sentenced him to death for high treason, but the officer in charge refused to carry out the order. Smith and a few others stewed in jail for a few months until they – probably with the help of one of the jailors – were able to escape and flee to Illinois.

The conflict reached its logical end in 1844. The Mormons had once again set up their own militia and once again Smith and his big brother Hyrum were arrested. One night, an armed mob with faces painted black stormed the jail in Carthage, Illinois and fired shots into the cells. Hyrum fell dead immediately. Joseph jumped to the window, where they shot him. His final words were, "Oh Lord, my God."

Today we look back and say: Joseph Smith preached polygamy, no wonder people hated him.

But Mormon polygamy was not well known at that time. There were rumors, but Smith mostly succeeded in keeping his marriages secret. Mormons were generally known as "polygamist" only later, when they openly practiced it in Utah.

The persecution began the moment the Book of Mormon was published.

I believe that was the real reason people hated him. I believe people back then recognized what we today do not: how radical the Book of Mormon is.

Traditional Christians ridicule the idea that Jesus visited the Americas as the bizarre ranting of a megalomaniacal fraud. For as long I was a church member, I heard that ridicule so often that I began wondering why people made such a big fuss about it. All religions make outlandish claims. If you believe Jesus rose from the dead and ascended into heaven, it's no big leap to believe that he spent three days among the American Indians, who, after all, are people too. The reason for all the scoffing can only be because people feel threatened.

As they should.

In the early 19th century, America was still very small and young, a cultural backwater, a reservoir for Europe's poor and disenfranchised. Spiritually, it was very much an appendage of Europe: Every American church, from the Catholics to the Lutherans, from the Methodists to the Baptists, was a subsidiary of a European denomination.

The Book of Mormon blatantly and unapologetically rejected this status quo and offered an alternative. Christianity in America no longer had to be imported from Rome or Wittenberg or Geneva or London, because Mormonism came to America straight from the source – from Jerusalem. Mormon Christianity was no poor distant cousin of European Christianity, it was an equal.

When Joseph Smith preached that Christ had visited America, he was preaching that the hundreds of American denominations based on European traditions didn't have a reason to exist. Just as early Christianity was designed to replace Judaism, Joseph Smith's American Christianity aimed to supplant the European monopoly on Christian thought. It was always easy for Methodists to live side by side with Congregationalists, because as variations of the same idea they had more in common than not, but Smith's ideas threatened them both to the very core. With a threat like that, every believing American understood in his heart that it was in the best interests of his European-based church to destroy the idea of a purely American religion before it took root.

That, I believe, is why Joseph Smith had to die.

By rights, with Joseph Smith out of the picture, his church should have dissolved.

Smith was a charismatic leader, a 19th-century Christian guru neither men nor women could resist, and a brilliant theologian as well. Among his followers, no one could walk in his shoes. At the time of his death, the "Mormon church" was really the Joseph Smith church.

What saved it was, ironically, the persecution.

When you're being attacked from all sides, you don't think too much about whether the guru's successor is as good as the original guru. You have more important things to worry about. The most urgent question facing the remaining church leaders was how to save their some 26,000 members from injury, dispossession and death.

The man who came up with the answer was not as sexy as Smith, but he did happen to be an organizational genius.

Brigham Young was four years older than Smith and was among the earliest converts to the church. The trained carpenter and blacksmith earned his money as an itinerant handyman and as a convert he continued to wander – as a missionary to Canada and England. When, following some political infighting, he was named Smith's prophet-successor, he announced a radical solution to the problem of persecution: The church would simply leave the United States.

Young himself pressed ahead with a small group of exiles. They traveled into Indian territory outside the reach of the US government, and with the help of Indians and fur traders eventually found a place that was so far away and so little coveted that Young could be sure no one would come out there and bother them: Mexico. But when I say "Mexico," I don't mean the Mexico of today, south of Texas – I mean the vast territory that stretched as far north as Canada.

Young went about preparing the journey with scientific precision. He had to figure out: Is a journey that far with so many people even possible? How would they survive the winter – so great a distance was impossible to cross without enduring at least one winter, no matter when you started. Where would they settle and what would they need to survive there?

Young meticulously recorded everything he observed and translated it into data, then delegated assignments to other travelers. He had someone count number of rotations a wagon wheel along the way: When the member assigned the job got tired of staring at a revolving piece of wood, he invented a device to do the work for him and called it a *Roadometer*. According to that invention, the average wagon wheel rotated 360 times per mile and in most cases the wagon progressed only some 2.25 miles per day. In total, the journey from Nauvoo, Illinois to Salt Lake City was some 3,100 miles long and would take more than 500 days, depending on weather, health and the length of the winter break.

Over the next thirteen years, an estimated 70,000 Mormons in various groups made the uncertain migration into unsettled Mexico. This was before the railroad, and the financial means of many church members were limited. Many converts were migrating from Europe – they were often poor and had spent most of their money on the voyage across the Atlantic. While some members could afford covered wagons and a team of oxen, others had to make the journey pushing or pulling a handcart.

A list published back then of goods that every family should bring along in order to survive on the road, as well as the first year in Utah, included such items as: two or three pair of oxen, two milk cows, other animals, weapons and ammunition, 15 pounds of metal, ropes and winches, fishing and farming equipment, 1,000 pounds of flour and more. Many members misjudged how many personal possessions they could take, and their ox teams got slower every day. You could always recognize the so-called "Mormon Trail" by the personal belongings that had been discarded for weight along the way – books, china, family heirlooms and furniture. One family wrapped their piano in buffalo hide and buried it, then came back years later and dug it up again.

Many didn't make it – especially those who weren't good at reading instructions and started the journey in late fall, which put them on the road when winter struck. One estimate puts the number of dead along the trail between 4,000 and 6,000.

And when the migrants finally reached their destination, they found themselves surrounded by desert.

Utah consists mainly of sand, rocks and mountains and an enormous solitary lake, and that is where Young built his headquarters. The water is beautiful, but it was named "Salt Lake" because it really is a salt-water lake. Fish cannot survive in it and the water is not usable for irrigation. Not even the Indians had been able to make Utah livable. But for Young, the challenge of living there was more attractive than constantly being shot at in the USA.

Brigham Young was one of these guys who really shine when they have an impossible job to perform. In very little time, he constructed a functioning irrigation system, designed cities, streets, shops and companies as well as the necessary laws. Utah's capital Salt Lake City is famous for streets arranged in a grid – Young designed the entire town by drawing vertical and horizontal lines on paper. He even included a little something for himself: For those of his 55 wives who bore him children, he built a house in which each of them had her own bedroom with a separate entrance and only one key, which she kept in her possession. With no false modesty whatsoever he christened his dwelling "Lion House."

But there was no escaping the US. While the migration was still underway, America attacked Mexico and snatched the entire land between the Rio Grande and Canada. All of a sudden Mormon Utah, as well as all the surrounding territories the Mormons had begun expanding into – were American. Immediately, persecution began anew.

The government in Washington didn't just have a problem with polygamy, it had a problem with Brigham Young himself, for he ruled his desert empire like a genuine theocrat. When the Mormon controversy once again boiled over back east, the president named a governor of Utah to replace Young and sent him out west accompanied by 2,500 soldiers.

Exactly what the soldiers' mandate was in Utah, the Mormons did not know. Nor did they know that the troops had instructions not to shoot. The Mormons only knew that soldiers were coming. Panic spread and rumors flew until the Mormons were convinced the army was going to kill them all. It appears Young made a decision: This time, they would stand their ground.

That was unfortunate for a harmless, barely armed group of pioneers known as the Baker-Fancher party, which around that time arrived in Utah from Arkansas. They were not Mormons – they were just passing through, heading for California. But the closer the group came, the stronger the rumors about it grew until many Mormons were convinced that they were only pretending to be pioneers, but were in fact the first group of soldiers.

Disguised as Indians so they could not be identified, the Mormons attacked the Baker-Fancher party in Mountain Meadows – and with horrifying determination slaughtered some 130 defenseless pioneers. Only the children under seven years were left alive.

The Mormons had plenty of experience with violence and death, but to murder 130 innocents, including women and children, was shocking not only to the Americans in the east, it turned the stomachs of the Mormons out west as well.

The soldiers soon arrived on the scene and instigated an investigation, but the Civil War intervened and their efforts petered out. In the end, only one Mormon leader was executed and the role played by Brigham Young in the "Mountain Meadows Massacre" remains unclear even today: It is possible he gave the command himself.

I never liked Brigham Young. I don't think he was a nice guy. I think he was a bully. He was too strict, too intolerant, too uncompromising, a hawk, a patriarch, probably an egomaniac, maybe a bigot, certainly not open to liberal values, like one of those hard-ass World War II generals who just can't comprehend that the soldiers on the other side love their children too; like the father who insists his kids address him as "sir;" like one of those fanatical Irish Catholic nuns who like to beat sensitive young men, who then grow up to become great suffering poets. I just don't like that kind of people.

But who else would have had the guts to attempt something that had never been attempted before, even though he was completely unqualified to do it, even though he knew he was risking the lives of his followers? Brigham Young had no reason to believe he would succeed. He had never trekked across this much unknown territory before, he had no idea how to organize thousands of people and keep them fed and safe, he had no idea how to design a city from scratch, much less an entire society.

But the one thing he did know, almost certainly, was that everything Joseph Smith had accomplished would have vanished in an instant if he didn't act.

Utopias in America pop up like weeds and get pulled out just as fast. That thing called Mormonism was at its core nothing more than an idea, and ideas are fragile, especially ideas that fly in the face of everything mainstream society accepts as true. And here was Brigham Young, with this bizarre idea dropped into his lap, an idea he was willing to die for and perhaps even kill for.

He only knew he had to do something. So he did.

It is a miracle that the entire project did not end in catastrophe. But the opposite happened: Brigham Young became recognized and respected in his own lifetime as governor of a new US territory, as founder of a state wondrously raised from desert sand and as the savior of his people from endless persecution. More importantly: He took a small, infamous cult and made it into a confident and determined religion that was able to withstand any attack.

The final words of this "American Moses," as he is sometimes called, as he died in 1877 at the age of 76 in his Lion House, were, "Joseph! Joseph! Joseph!"

CHAPTER 2

Eisenhowerland

THE FIRST TIME I HEARD ABOUT POLYGAMY, I DIDN'T believe it. I was about twelve or thirteen. It was during one of those phases when my parents had a little money. They decided to send their kids to a better school, so they picked out a private school with a good reputation run by the Seventh-day Adventists. The curriculum there included Bible study, which, by the way, wasn't quite as Seventh-day Adventist-y as you might expect: Kids from all kinds of churches attended, so religion had to be at least a little impartial. But once in a while, the regular religion teacher would get sick and the local pastor substituted. Thus it happened that said pastor one day decided to explain to us all what kind of bizarre and morally despicable theological aberrations churches other than the Seventh-day Adventists believed in. The Mormons were featured prominently. Mormons, he claimed, until very recently, had practiced polygamy. Of course, he had to explain what polygamy was.

There was no way I was taking that sitting down.

I got up and told him it wasn't true and I knew because I was a Mormon and we don't marry several wives nor do anything like that and we never will and never did and he was lying. At first, he stuck to his guns, but I wouldn't shut up. I contradicted every word that came out his mouth, and I kept it up the whole hour until the poor man finally gave up, desperate, and admitted that maybe he had misunderstood something.

I was still furious when I got home. Outraged, I reported the scandal to my mother and was surprised when she seemed more puzzled than upset. She turned to me and said, "But sweetheart, didn't you know? Of course we used to practice polygamy."

The 19th century was a time when everyone was rediscovering the Bible. You read the Bible and stumbled across some verse that had long been forgotten and the very fact that it was forgotten made it suddenly seem more important than ever. That's how the Seventh-day Adventists discovered that Sunday is the first day of the week, not the seventh, and so they built a denomination based on going to church on Saturday; the Jehovah's Witnesses discovered that eating blood was forbidden and outlawed blood sausage and, later, transfusions; the German New Apostolic Church noticed that Jesus had twelve apostles and designed their organization based on that tidbit.

No one can tell me that of all these hard-working Bible scholars, only Joseph Smith noticed that in the Old Testament Abraham, Jacob, David and Solomon had multiple wives. Everyone knew it, but only Joseph Smith had the guts to say, "Hey, look what I found."

In the beginning, Smith was cautious. Though he married an estimated 34 women, for most of his life he kept the practice as secret as possible. Polygamy didn't become the primary attribute of Mormonism until Brigham Young, in the safety of Utah, lived openly with his 55 wives and 56 children and assigned additional wives to about 30 percent of the male members of the church he deemed worthy and capable.

Some aspects of Mormon polygamy remain puzzling even today.

For example the question: Did Smith believe that polygamy was a divine commandment, or could he just not keep it in his pants?

By all accounts, Smith was not a buttoned-down guy, and the claim that he was a philanderer would certainly fit his personality. That impression is underscored by the oft-made observation that some of his wives were pretty and would today be considered underage (the youngest was 14, the oldest 58). And it appears that he hid his activities from his first wife. It seems reasonable to assume that sex played a role in his motivation.

On the other hand, if this was only about sex, why do are there doubts that he even consummated all his marriages? Though Smith had eleven children with his first wife, few or possibly no children were conceived with his 30-plus additional wives: Posthumous DNA tests reveal that of the nine children from his polygamous marriages, five were not his (some of his wives were simultaneously married to other men) and the four remaining tests were inconclusive. On top of that, 20 of his wives were married to him "for eternity" – which implies that the marriage would only be valid after death, and he would be expected to keep his hands off them here on earth. A few wives were even married to him posthumously.

Even Brigham Young – he of the 56 children and the Lion House – seems not to have had sex with all his wives. Some of them were simultaneously married to other men and at least six marriages were explicitly "for eternity" only. Only 16 of his wives bore him children.

There are a handful of theories about how and why Mormon polygamy came to be.

Feminists put forth the reasonable idea that polygamy was a tool to strengthen the church's patriarchal structure. Sociologists and historians discuss other theories. For example, security: Mormons in Utah had significantly more women than men, and because women on their own had few rights at that time, they needed the security of marriage to survive. Others see polygamy as a practical means of increasing membership: Because only "worthy" men were assigned additional wives, polygamy produced large families that remained close to the church.

I suspect there is some truth to all these theories. My favorite is another, however: the marketplace.

If you wanted to make a name for yourself in the crowded marketplace of religions (and not only back then), you had to offer something no one else could. If all you did was repeat the familiar teachings of the established churches, why should anyone take notice? But if you could outlaw the eating of blood sausage or switch church services from Sunday to Saturday, people would start talking about you. And if you managed to interpret Christianity in a completely new way, the entire nation would talk about you.

Unusual doctrines don't just grab attention, they define the kind of follower you get. Radical teachings attract radicals – people who are willing to do anything for their convictions. If you're the sort of believer who thinks it's enough to attend Sunday services, you're not going to follow a prophet from state to state and then into the desert, but that was the kind of believer Joseph Smith needed.

With polygamy, he turned generally accepted social norms upside down, which must have attracted the attention of the most radical of believers. If any religious founder ever practiced the American ideal of "thinking big," it was Smith.

Mormon polygamy only lasted about 40 years, but American society is still dealing with the fallout.

In 1890, the then-prophet and president of the church received the divine revelation that polygamy would cease to be a doctrine. But it wasn't God alone who made that decision. The newest batch of laws from the federal government was making polygamy more and more difficult. At the same time, the US baited the church by promising that if it banned polygamy, the territory of Utah would become a state. By this time, statehood was a promising prospect. As a state, Utah would gain significant political and economic advantages. So polygamy was banned and six years later Utah officially joined the US.

Some members left the church in protest and formed their own sects. They had suffered years of persecution for their beliefs, and all of a sudden God just changes his mind? Clearly, church leadership had strayed from the true path. Today, an estimated 40,000 "fundamentalist Mormons" live in the US and Canada as polygamists in various religious groupings.

At first, the government did its best to enforce anti-polygamy laws, but in the meantime society has changed so much that polygamy is impossible to outlaw.

A good example is Short Creek, Arizona:

In 1953 some 100 police officers stormed the compound of a small polygamous community there. Unfortunately, the 400 or so polygamists knew the police were coming. They also knew the press would be there. The day after the raid, photos appeared in the newspapers. Alas, no one saw photos of grateful, frightened women being saved from perverted sex games, but they did see police handcuffing harmless, peacefully singing Christian families and herding them into buses.

The biggest problem was the children. Polygamous families have a lot of kids. What do you do with them while their parents are in prison? When the police in Short Creek separated 263 children from their parents, public opinion went from outrage over polygamy to outrage over a government that would torture those innocent young ones. In the next election, the governor of Arizona – who had rather showily promised to cleanse the state of polygamy – was driven out of politics.

The more our attitudes toward sex change, the more difficult it is to prosecute polygamy, and since the 19th century our attitudes have changed enormously.

Today, if you experiment a little with "free love" or with an "open marriage," you are considered sexually progressive. There's even a modest movement among some young people today called "polyamory" – love to more than one person at the same time. No one gets upset about that.

But people still do get upset when you use the word "polygamy," mostly out of tradition, I think. Polygamy comes from a time before "free love," when people were genuinely outraged by it, and today we have inherited that outrage along with the term. If polygamous Mormons today were to open up a chain of over-expensive coffee shops and vinyl record stores and claim they were living a "social-sexual experiment," we would call them hipsters and engage in long, overly serious discussions about polygamy and polyandry (one woman, multiple husbands) as the future of our society.

The laws, too, have changed with the times.

Starting in 2010, the reality show *Sister Wives* began depicting the life of Kody Brown and his four wives and 18 children, all of them seemingly normal and relatively happy. The general attorney's office was watching too, and soon Brown found himself facing charges of polygamy. He thought he had a good case, however, as he had legally only married his first wife; the others were living with him without a marriage license. The law says you can't legally marry twice at the same time, but there is no law against sharing your house, bed and family with more than one partner at the same time, as long as you're not legally married. From a legal perspective, Brown argued, polygamy is the same thing as a married man keeping a mistress. Fooling around isn't illegal.

In 2013, the court decided in Brown's favor: The government, it said, can limit your legal marriages to one, but it has no right to tell you who you can or can't sleep with. For all intents and purposes, polygamy is now legal in the US.

You might think the Mormon church is happy about that, but it is not. Now that the church has become part of the religious mainstream, its earlier radicalism has mutated into ironclad conservatism, and it is the only large institution that still actively fights polygamy.

Visiting a Mormon church for Sunday church services today is akin to time travel.

You feel like you have entered a kind of Disneyland for the prosperous white middle class of yesteryear, an Eisenhower-era time-bubble where everything is just like those commercials in glossy magazines of the '50s and '60s:

Two cars in the garage, three kids, the boys with short hair, Dad in a tie or mowing the lawn or washing the car, Mom in a petticoat in her state-of-the-art kitchen stirring up something nice. Smiling, of course, and with perfect teeth. Father has a good job, he is employed and maybe in middle management or he runs his own business, he is head of the family, respected and always there for them. Mom runs the household and watches over the kids and supports Dad. She exudes happiness, warmth and security, she takes care of the family's social affairs. The children are happy, balanced, behaved, focused on education and sports, full of energy and sometimes they're little rascals, but clearly a grand future is awaiting them.

What a spectacular utopia! Who wouldn't want to live like that? My heart is overflowing just writing these lines. The Eisenhower family is a stranger to crime, war, poverty and severe diseases. In this perfect suburb, the dangers of modern life stay outside. That is the unspoken promise of the church: If you come to us, we will help you build the ideal family life.

And the church is surprisingly good at providing its members with that kind of life, or something very close to it.

Thanks to their very specific commandments and intense community involvement, life in the church holds far fewer risks than life outside. If you want to live in a world without unwanted teenage pregnancies, you forbid premarital sex. Want a lower divorce rate? Outlaw extramarital sex and stress the importance of the family every chance you get. You want a well-organized, middle-class and financially well-off society? Preach the values of education, hard work and obedience to the law – constantly. It works.

Of course Mormons are subject to crime, alcoholism, sexual confusion, divorce, poverty, sickness and all the rest of it – but the church with its commandments, tightly-knit social structure and constant admonitions from the pulpit manages to keep all that to a minimum. If you do everything the church tells you, your chances of getting through life with far fewer of these terrible things are pretty good.

Take alcohol and cigarettes. In 1833, Joseph Smith received a revelation from God called "The Word of Wisdom," which instructs Mormons to shun alcohol, coffee, tobacco and any form of drugs. Ironically, outsiders sneer at those goody-goody Mormons for their prudishness, even though everyone knows alcohol and tobacco are two of the biggest causes of death and disease in our society. In truth, the Word of Wisdom makes Mormons healthier than the average health nut, fitness freak, organic and local food fanatic, vegetarian or vegan. Every once in a while a study comes out that compares the health situations of various religions. Again and again, these studies show that Mormons are the second-most healthiest religious group in the US just after the Seventh-day Adventists (who, in addition to similar health laws, outlaw meat).

One might think that with so much prudishness, many incredibly healthy Mormons would lose their desire to live, yet studies also show that the suicide rate among active Mormons is up to three times lower than among non-Mormons. And these studies don't stop at the Word of Wisdom – they often name less easily measurable factors like a stable family life, high education, intense spirituality and high idealism among Mormons.

There's another advantage faithful church members have: Mormons tend to be successful.

Since the USA was founded, when the first hungry immigrants got off the boat, an ideology of personal advancement was intimately interwoven into the fabric of the American soul. Once the American was freed from the rigid hierarchy of European feudalism, in which no one was ever meant to rise above the station God assigned to him – from that moment on, to be American was to strive to make something out of your life, to advance yourself socially and financially; Americans are meant to strive for personal success and by striving to become better human beings.

The origin of the American doctrine of success goes back 200 years before the American Revolution, to the Puritans who founded New England and have influenced the nation's culture enormously ever since. It was from the Calvinists that the Puritans inherited the idea that you could please God by sheer diligence. Both Calvinists and Puritans worked to save their souls, and they worked hard. For them, idleness and pleasure were open invitations to Satan to snatch up their souls. But if you wasted none of your time on Earth, you could escape Lucifer's temptations.

The visible evidence that you were diligent was success. It makes sense: If you work hard, you are bound to see the fruits of your labor eventually. That was true also for money: Profit was often considered to be the natural reward for a God-fearing life. Historians who research the accounting books of Puritan shopkeepers often find scrawled in the margins phrases like: "In the name of God and in the name of profits."

Europeans, in my experience, tend to see wealth differently. Coming from a feudal system, they are used to associating money with nobility, which is not earned by hard work but is a birthright. In feudal times, if you were rich but not of noble lineage, there was something suspicious about your wealth – maybe you were a merchant, who cheats his customers, or even worse, a Jew. Even today, Europeans still tend to find wealth somehow unsavory, as a sign that you have a skeleton in your closet somewhere. In Germany – one of the wealthiest, most successful capitalist countries in the world – I constantly detect a deep moral and psychological mistrust toward people who strive for profit or success. They are considered shallow, corrupt and soulless. Both Marxism and Hitler's National Socialism were driven by a frantic mistrust, even fear of capitalism and of the people who understand how it works.

In post-Puritan America, it's the other way around: If you are satisfied with what you have and display no desire to strive for more, you are considered passive and subservient. Success is considered proof that someone is exceptionally intelligent, hardworking and morally on the level.

In 1890 Russell Conwell, a Baptist preacher and the founder of Temple University in Philadelphia, composed a speech entitled *Acres of Diamonds* that became so popular, he ended up giving it 6,000 times. In it, he exhorted fellow Americans, "It is your duty to become rich. The men who get rich may be the most honest men you will find in the community. Let me say here clearly, ninety-eight out of one hundred of the rich men of America are honest. That is why they are rich. That is why they are trusted with money."

Today, too, in bestsellers like *How to Win Friends & Influence People,* by Dale Carnegie; *Think and Grow Rich* by Napoleon Hill; *The Secret* by Rhonda Byrne and *The 7 Habits of Highly Effective People: Powerful Lessons in Personal Change* by the Mormon Stephen R. Covey, making money is depicted not only as a good idea financially but as a personal and moral triumph as well.

While for Germans, rich men like Bill Gates are considered dangerous and corrupt, most Americans see them as exceptionally intelligent, maybe even wise. Bill Gates dedicated his entire life to computers and business, and that's what he knows best – yet, if he were to write a book about the search for spiritual fulfillment, it would be a bestseller, even though that is clearly not the area of his expertise.

The famous Protestant work ethic is nowhere more celebrated than in the Mormon church. When I was young, hardly a day – or a church meeting – went by when I wasn't confronted in some subtle or not so subtle way with the ideology of success: "You can become anything you want," "Anything is possible," "Practice makes perfect." The dogma "You must follow your dreams" is part of Mormon culture like the noodle casserole Mormon women make for sick neighbors. It's even embedded in the hymns Mormons sing every Sunday.

Most songs in the Mormon hymnal are English Protestant hymns from the 18th and 19th centuries – songs that are sung in practically every Protestant church in England and America today. Many of these, *Onward, Christian Soldiers* or Luther's *A Mighty Fortress Is Our God,* were written in Europe during the violent persecution of the Protestant movements and are stridently militaristic – they describe religious life as a battle that must inevitably be won. Others are hymns of comfort and reassurance in times of hardship, for example, *How Firm a Foundation,* which promises, "Fear not, I am with thee; oh, be not dismayed, For I am thy God and will still give thee aid."

Then there is a handful of hymns written by the Mormons themselves. One stands out as "more Mormon" than any other: *Come, Come Ye Saints,* written during the journey West (coincidentally, by the same man who invented the Roadometer). It quickly became the unofficial hymn of the Mormon Trail and today is the unofficial Mormon anthem, but if you look closer at the lyrics, the hymn actually has little to do with religion.

Instead, it conjures up the hardships of the journey and encourages members never to give up:

> Why should we mourn or think our lot is hard?
> 'Tis not so; all is right.
> Why should we think to earn a great reward
> If we now shun the fight?
> Gird up your loins; fresh courage take.
> Our God will never us forsake;
> And soon we'll have this tale to tell —
> All is well! All is well!

The text is about following your dream against all odds, never giving up no matter the difficulties, for God rewards the persistent with success.

It turned out to be right: The Mormons did get to Utah and succeeded in making a life there for themselves. *Come, Come Ye Saints* is not only the embodiment of the dogma of success; it is proof that the dogma is true.

Interestingly, the doctrine of success didn't start with America or even with the Calvinists. It goes all the way back to Jesus.

"For the kingdom of heaven is as a man traveling into a far country, who called his own servants, and delivered unto them his goods," begins the parable of the talents in the New Testament (Matthew 25:14–30). It goes on to tell the tale of three servants to whom the master gives money – "talents" – in various quantities to administer in his stead. The first two servants invest the money and turn varying profits, while the third fearfully buries the money so it can't get lost. When the master returns, he praises and rewards the first two servants who made a profit. The third servant, who had timidly decided against taking the risk of investment, is punished: "For unto every one that hath, shall be given, and he shall have abundance; but from him that hath not shall be taken away even that which he hath."

Mormons interpret this parable to mean that God has given us one life and expects us to make something out of it. If you do, you're living up to the expectations of your Creator. If not – if all we do is hold out until the end, steering clear of all risk – then we have shown contempt toward this unique, divine gift of life.

It's fashionable to equate the American dogma of success with greed or materialism, but that is a superficial interpretation. For Mormons, success is never success if it does not include happiness, personal and family fulfillment and a practically lived morality. When Mormons strive for success, it's always about living a fulfilled life. At the same time the "You can do it"-mentality is preached from the pulpit, members are constantly taught a specifically Mormon form of selflessness and generosity that is the opposite of greed and materialism. It starts with the lay priesthood.

With very few exceptions – secretaries, janitors, a handful of managers in the upper echelons who work full-time – no one in the church is paid. Sunday school teachers and the leaders of various other programs, the bishop (the Mormon equivalent of pastor), his bosses in the next levels up (stake presidents and others) – everyone who keeps Mormon life running – all work without pay. That's in addition to their full-time jobs as electricians and shop owners, cashiers and police, politicians and cooks. After they perform their duty in the church (their "calling") for three or four years, they are relieved, the job is assigned to the next member – and they receive a new calling.

Only "worthy" members are called to perform the essential duties – for Mormons, that tends to mean gainfully employed family fathers who work 40 hours or more a week and are already fighting to spend time with their families. I don't know anyone who works as hard as a typical Mormon bishop.

And without training. Not even the bishop with his organizational and pastoral responsibilities gets special training.

Or maybe they do: Members are integrated into the church workforce from when they are kids. They start with small jobs and work their way up. Young men receive the priesthood in their teens and with it they get assignments – administering the "sacrament" (the eucharist – Mormons use bread and water) at Sunday services, for example. Mormon teenagers are mini-priests.

Perhaps the most important aspect of the lay priesthood is the "talk" – the Sunday sermon.

You can't expect an overworked and unpaid bishop to write and hold a sermon every week. That job is delegated. On any given Sunday, three to four members, one after the other, will stand before the congregation and speak briefly about a subject they choose themselves or that is assigned by the bishop.

Even teenagers are assigned a "two and a half minute talk." It's the terror of growing up Mormon. You stand up there, trembling with fear, and read, haltingly and without raising your eyes, a short essay that you had worked on up to the wee hours of the morning, consisting of verses from the Bible or the Book of Mormon, a joke or a personal anecdote of some kind and maybe, if you're courageous, a half-hearted piece of wisdom from your own life. Before you, you see all the parents of the "ward" (the congregation) politely nodding their heads and smiling and remembering back to the time when they held their first two and a half minute talk. Afterward, they congratulate you: "You did very well." By the time an average Mormon has reached adulthood, he has no problem standing in front of a room of strangers and holding a presentation.

The church has enough money to pay professional priests, but the members would reject them. For Mormons, a professional priest is a corrupt priest. If you take money for serving God, you would probably also serve the Devil if he paid more.

On top of that, there is the idealism. Mormons are proud that their lives are not all about striving for money or fame or pleasure, or leisure time, but for the things they believe in: God, the truth, family and love, the good in mankind, doing the right thing. Those are themes that lay priests and other members preach every Sunday from the pulpit. Mormons are idealists.

Taking on unpaid jobs in the church is not the only way Mormons prove that they are Mormons. They also pay cash.

The endless willingness of Mormons to give away their money and even to torment themselves physically for their cause is best illustrated by "Fast Sunday:" On every first Sunday of the month, members go without eating (though they can drink water) for 24 hours or at least two full meals. (They are meant to use the extra time they gain to ruminate on their spiritual lives, but of course in practice most Mormons take the opportunity to get something done around the house that has been nagging at them for too long and to ruminate on how good that next meal is going to be.)

The money they save on groceries is collected and redistributed to needy church members. Fast Sunday is a relict of the quasi-communist beginnings of the church.

That's right: This most American of all churches flirted in its earliest phase with an idea that you could call "communism." Joseph Smith and others were convinced that the first Christians lived a communal lifestyle: Everyone pooled their money and only took out what they needed. While Karl Marx was sitting in London formulating his theses, Joseph Smith was already organizing his church "communally." Alas, it didn't work, and the idea was soon abandoned. But the idea that the members (who still today address each other as "brother" and "sister") are there for each other in a kind of extended family is still alive: No Mormon has ever had to hire movers; no Mormon ever had to cook for himself when he was sick.

The money that comes in on Fast Sunday flows into the massive Mormon welfare system that primarily finances needy members, but not only them. The church subsidiary "LDS Philanthropies" organizes and finances a series of charity and not-for-profit organizations that include universities and high schools in America, Mexico and the South Pacific. (When I was ready to attend college, I didn't have the money to go to the college I wanted, so I started out at the Brigham Young University in Hawaii, where admission was affordable for me as a member.) It also funds various projects all over the world that finance birth aid, wheelchairs, eye operations and water wells. In 2008, the church, according to its website, helped out in 124 catastrophes in 48 countries, and after Hurricane Katrina struck in 2005, Mormon trucks were famously among the first responders, before government relief arrived.

All that is not financed by Fast Sunday alone: Members are expected to donate the substantial sum of 10 percent of their income to the church.

According to the Old Testament, the Children of Israel gave a "tithe" or "tithing," defined as a "tenth," to the priests or the temple. That appears to be what inspired Joseph Smith to ask his followers to hand over 10 percent of their income. That's a lot of money – especially if you have a large family to feed.

Thanks to the combination of tithing and the lay priesthood, which keeps administration costs close to zero, the Mormon church is one of the richest in the world. *Bloomberg Businessweek* estimated in 2012 that the church takes in between seven and eight billion dollars a year and is worth about $40 billion. Some say only the Catholic Church is richer.

My non-Mormon friends are outraged when they hear that: How can a church so brazenly exploit its members?

There was a time when that got me upset too. Then I began to notice a certain difference between the average Mormon and the average non-member: materialism.

Mormons are achievement-driven, but their priorities are clearly not the accumulation of wealth or status symbols, nor do they make good hedonists. When I left the church, I expected to find most non-members just as generous, benevolent and idealistic as Mormons. I thought all that was normal. But outside the church I found these values to be relatively rare. It's not that non-members were evil or mean (that, too, I expected to find, and didn't), it's just that the average guy out there tends to think a little bit more of himself. Selflessness and idealism have to be learned, and the church teaches its members well.

Possibly the biggest personal sacrifice Mormons are asked to make is to go on a mission.

The Mormon church asks its young men of 19 to sacrifice two years of their lives to go out into the world and preach Mormonism to strangers (it also asks young women, but there's more pressure on boys to accept). And they do it on their own dime – the church doesn't pay a cent, not even the flight.

Kids who accept know what they are getting into. On a mission, they will have to abstain from practically everything they love – parties, friendships, family and romance. Their only contact with their families back home will be one letter a week. They will not be allowed to go to movies or watch TV during that time and the only music they can listen to is classic – the biggest sacrifice of all. They will have to dress conservatively – boys wear suits and ties every day and keep their hair short. They know they will often be jeered at on the street. They know they will face brutal rejection, even hate, on a daily basis. And they know when they return, all their friends and family will have moved on – they will be two years behind everyone else.

The church has only one argument why a young man should make such a sacrifice: If you believe, you will do it.

Somewhere between 30,000 and 40,000 kids accept the call every year.

It's common to complain about how superficial and selfish the kids of today are, brain-dead consumers of fast food, PlayStation games and Internet porn, but as a Mormon, I knew a great proportion of kids who were willing to sacrifice a significant chunk of their best years for what they believed in. (And they aren't the only ones: I think most kids out there would be willing to sacrifice their lives for something they believed in – if they were asked.)

The missionary program is the main reason why the church is growing so swiftly – there are now some 15 million members around the world, only about half of them in the United States.

But there is more to it than that. A mission is like the army – it makes a man out of you. You send away a kid, and what comes back is a young man or woman who has learned the value of hard work, determination, discipline and goals, to deal with rejection, to live 24 hours with a companion he didn't choose and possibly doesn't even like (missionaries always live and work in twos, for reasons of security and moral support), to deal diplomatically and personally with strangers, to know his or her strengths and limits, and often to speak a foreign language. These are the kids who continue all their lives to build up the church.

Like almost everything else in the church, the missionary program is designed not only to bring in new members, but to create a better human being. Just as Fast Sunday teaches young people the value of letting go of money, a mission teaches you the value of sacrificing your needs and desires for something greater than yourself. And if you think all this has less to do with theology than with lifestyle, you're right. From the beginning, Mormonism was only half meant to be a religion. The other half was a utopia.

Beginning with the Puritans of the 17th century up through the Amish of the 18th and all the way to hippie communes of the 1970s, America was always a breeding ground for utopian experiments. When Joseph Smith and his early followers built their own towns, institutions, laws and traditions, they were creating an alternative society where they could live the way God wanted them to and remain immune to the corrupting influence of the godless world outside.

This idea is still woven into the structure of Mormonism: The church dominates so much of members' lives that they hardly have time to fraternize with non-Mormons, much less get corrupted by them. This is intentional: Members are meant to stay as far from the temptation of the world as possible. Of course, Mormons live alongside non-Mormons and have non-Mormon friends. But Mormon commandments, from the Word of Wisdom to the laws governing sexual behavior, are so prominent that non-members will always treat members as strangers and never let them into their lives completely – and that makes it easier for Mormons to avoid the temptations of their non-believing friends. When I went to high school, the grown-ups often warned me to avoid drugs and sex and never to give into peer pressure, but those cautions were unnecessary – my friends knew I was a Mormon and kept their sinful ways hidden from me. If there were such things as wild drug and sex parties in my high school, no one invited me.

There is a downside to all this. Mormonism isn't for everyone, and it took me a long time growing up to realize that I might be one of those other people.

First, there was the boredom.

Speaking in church, Mormons have a naturally limited number of subjects to choose from, and if you grow up attending meetings each Sunday, by the time you're a teenager you've heard them all. The time Sister Brown's prayers were answered. How Brother Hendrickson got his testimony. A couple dozen favorite verses from the Bible or the Book of Mormon and how they apply to our lives as husbands and wives and mothers and fathers. Admonitions to pray every day, to read the scriptures regularly, to love your spouse. Sister Mortonson's family problems. The time Brother Jackson didn't have the money to pay his tithing, but paid it anyway and found a hundred dollar bill lying on the sidewalk and could meet his rent at the end of the month.

All of it very heartfelt and emotional – these are real people talking about their real lives – but still, it gets old. Church attendance in general deeply defined my life, but my memories of actual church services are mostly about fighting to stay awake, my head falling to my chest and jerking forward again with a start. And of course trying to smuggle comic books and science fiction novels into Sunday meetings. When my parents figured out why I wanted to sit apart from the family in the back row, that ended quickly.

To be fair, I should mention that after I left the church, I visited a couple of Catholic and Lutheran services, out of curiosity. I'd like to be able to report that they were more interesting, but if anything, they were duller. Boredom seems to be a universal experience of attending church.

Then there was youth division's focus on sports.

In addition to Sunday services, Mormon teenagers head back to church one more night a week to listen to a brief lesson and engage in some kind of social activity – just the kids, together. The Mutual Improvement Association (MIA) is meant to offer teens an interesting and engaging alternative to running around with non-Mormon kids, who will seduce them into taking drugs and engaging in premarital sex. But in practice, the social activity offered every week was basketball.

That made sense: Sports are healthy, especially in an age of television, and in a church that brings together so many different people with so many diverse backgrounds and interests, finding a common denominator, especially for the youth, was always a problem. And most kids liked sports. Except me. I was the nerd in the corner reading fantasy and science fiction novels while the other kids picked teams.

My poor MIA teachers didn't know what to do with me. Every once in a while, one of them would sit down with me and ask what I liked to do, and I would say I liked to read, and he would say, "Yeah, but I mean with other kids, in a group?" And I said, a little naively, and perhaps with a bit too much hope in my voice, "We could all read together," and that was that.

But they tried.

Then there was the thing with writing. I wanted to be a writer. That was a conflict.

The Mormon church encourages education and intellectual activity of any kind, and the goal of becoming a writer was certainly an honorable one, but what no one told me is that you can't write and be a Mormon at the same time.

There is a little known but stubborn strain of thought in the Protestant tradition that fiction is bad for you. It goes like this: When evil is depicted in novels and drama, it automatically becomes attractive. The Devil, the criminal and the fornicator are more interesting than the goody-goody. Even if they get their comeuppance in the end, they are always cool. By its very nature, fiction makes evil attractive, especially to the young reader.

Puritans and other Calvinist strains of Protestantism, particularly in Europe before the 18th century, repeatedly forbade drama and novels for those reasons, and the sentiment has survived until today. As a kid, one of my favorite movies was *Camelot*, and I remember talking about it to a Mormon friend – it turned out his father wouldn't let him see it because it "glorified" infidelity. When I was attending the Seventh-Day Adventist school, to meet state requirements it had to teach literature, but the teacher would regularly preface his lectures with a reminder that we should actually not read novels at all and that the founder of the Seventh-Day Adventists thought fiction in general was evil.

Protestant churches don't take that idea very seriously anymore, but it still pops up in ways we don't immediately recognize as Puritanical:

We disapprove of cigarettes in movies because it encourages the young to smoke. We don't like the use of the "N-word" even in historical novels because it appears to normalize racism. I remember when the excellent war movie about the final days of the Third Reich came out, *Downfall*, a lot of critics in Germany condemned it for depicting Hitler humanly. They were right, of course: Bruno Ganz's brilliant portrayal of Hitler was deeply human – before seeing the movie, you imagined Hitler something like a comic book villain; afterward, you realized that he could just as easily have been your creepy uncle. And every mass shooting or other violent spectacle immediately inspires calls for a ban on violent movies and video games. And of course political correctness, defined as an attempt to change the language to reflect not what life is, but what it should be, is also an expression of Puritanism.

All that is an echo of the Calvinist fear of fiction. If you believe the true purpose of literature is to instruct and improve the reader, you are at heart a Puritan.

As a Mormon, I was a Puritan in many ways, but I also believed the purpose of literature (and journalism) was to depict and explore the world and humanity as it is, not as it should be.

That was my dilemma.

Mormonism is a recipe for returning to God, much like a cookie recipe is a recipe for cookies. You follow the recipe correctly, you will return to God. Thus, a large part of Mormonism consists of members encouraging each other to conform to a certain standard of behavior and thinking. Both inwardly and outwardly, Mormons strive to force human nature into an ideal mold. A Mormon does not try to understand human nature, he certainly does not celebrate it, he tries to change it.

A certain amount of conformity is not a bad thing. In any society, you are expected to conform to the law, for example, or society won't work. If you are part of an orchestra setting out to play Beethoven's Ninth, but instead of playing the notes on the sheet, you indulge in wild, individualistic improvisations, no one praises you for breaking the mold.

But for a writer, conformism is not so good.

I knew that to become a writer would take a huge effort. I would have to make it my highest goal. Even that was a conflict, for God had a different idea about what my highest goal should be: To become a good person.

You can say there's no conflict between wanting to be a writer and wanting to be a good person – after all, a writer can be a good person too – but that's naive. Being a good person in the Mormon sense means constantly fighting against the ugliness of the world. That battle becomes your inner life. You live in a moral ivory tower, and what you see of the world, you judge. When you see the world as right or wrong, you end up writing a tract about right and wrong. As a teenager, starting out, I found my stories tended to end up looking very much like moral lectures. If a character's heart was not in the right place, he got his comeuppance in the end. But that's not what happens in the real world. The real world often turns out to be exactly what we don't want. Try as I might, I could not get my writing to reflect what was really out there. Even when the stories were about elves battling dragons, I was actually writing about the importance of being a good Mormon.

I noticed the difference most clearly after I left the church.

At the time, I was living in Munich, and I liked to hang out with some non-member friends. They were ex-pats from California, mostly. We would sit around talking about books and movies and our families and Germany and why we ended up here. But when it was late and I went home, I was always aware that they stayed on. As if the second part of the evening could begin once I was gone. They had something together that they couldn't share with me.

That was before I left the church. Afterwards, something strange happened.

One night, we were in my little place, I had cooked for them, it was getting late and the others went silent. They cast looks at each other, silently asking questions they didn't want me to hear. One nodded to the other, a third grinned, someone laughed and pulled out a joint.

I had not known about that part of their lives before. They had kept it a strict secret from me. They knew I was a Mormon and didn't want to scare me off. Only now could they show more of themselves.

Deep inside, I must have known I would have to make a decision someday. I succeeded in tamping it down and putting it off, but it hung in my soul like an ever-growing weight and turned my dreams sour. It took until I was about thirty before I could bring myself to admit that I could never write truthfully and be a Mormon.

The Eisenhower Era is over, but no one told the Mormons. Like Don Quixote fighting windmills, Mormons stubbornly hold onto the '50s utopia while everyone around them has long since revised their perspective on that period. The idyllic, prosperous '50s were fine for middle-class whites, but for a large percentage of the population, it was a living nightmare. Blacks were practically enslaved under Jim Crow laws, homosexuality was considered such a perversion that gays were forced to lead nearly invisible lives, women were often considered sexual objects and baby machines and were scorned if they wanted more than just the role of mother.

Today, despite occasional setbacks, the world is moving toward a vision of society-wide inclusion. Yet the Mormon church remains firmly patriarchal, anti-homosexual and, though it does not discriminate based on color, it is still hobbled by a history of discrimination and at least in the US is clearly oriented toward white middle-class society.

For the most American of all religions, that's disheartening. To imagine that God rejects entire groups of people flies in the face of everything America is about – the country was founded on the radical idea of equal chance and the right of all men to pursue happiness. More than any other religion, Mormonism preaches free will and personal progression – yet it indirectly denies these principles to women, gays and much of non-white society.

That was less noticeable when the church was on the fringes of society, but that, too, has changed: Since Mitt Romney, a Mormon, had a realistic chance of winning the White House, the public has become far more aware and accepting of Mormonism as a legitimate religion. And the more people watch, the more they criticize, loudly. As society churns forward, the church has stubbornly dug in, in a misguided and desperate attempt to return to values that are outdated. But the pressure to change is mounting, and it cannot hold out forever.

I remember one Sunday in June 1978 when a man no one in our family knew came home with us after church for dinner. Fried chicken or pork chops, I would guess: Either one would have been a typical Sunday dinner for my mother. The occasion was unusual for several reasons.

First, my parents were not the most sociable people in the world. It was rare to have guests over, much less for dinner. Second, the awkwardness. We didn't know this guy, had nothing in common with him and had nothing to talk about. My parents did their best to make small talk, and so did he, but none of them was good at it and the conversation was punctuated by long unhappy silences in which my siblings and I endured crippling embarrassment for Mom and Dad.

Third, the man was black.

It's hard to imagine how shocking it was that Sunday in June 1978 when the church leaders announced that effective immediately, blacks would no longer be excluded from holding the priesthood. We were confused. Our bishop had to explain exactly what it meant: For the first time in Mormon history, black males would have the same opportunities and privileges in the priesthood as white males.

But that didn't mean they could hold offices in the priesthood, did it?

Yes, it meant blacks could hold any priesthood office that a white man could hold. They would be just like whites.

But not the important offices, like bishop, right?

Yes, all offices, including the office of bishop and all other higher positions. Just like whites.

But not president, right? The president of the church is the prophet. He talks with God, when necessary. A black still could not become president and prophet of the church and talk with God, could he?

Yes, he could.

That day after church, my father walked up to the only black man in the congregation, who was as shell-shocked as we were, and invited him over for dinner.

From the early days of Joseph Smith and Brigham Young, blacks had been invited to join the church, yet excluded from holding the priesthood. When members asked why, we were generally told it was because of the "Mark of Cain."

You will recall that in the Bible, Cain slew his brother Abel and was cursed by God with a curse that would extend to all his descendants. An old theory, which became popular in America during the 19th century to justify slavery, said that the Mark of Cain was black skin. Though a lot of churches in America were racist for a long time, the Mormons were one of the few who used the Mark of Cain to block blacks from holding the priesthood.

That meant not only could black members not hold offices of responsibility in the church, which all other boys started doing as teens, they could not perform acts of priesthood in the home, like "blessing" their wives and children in times of sickness and crisis. A "blessing" is when a priesthood-holder lays his hands on the head of someone and prays, blessing him or her in the name of God and by the power of the priesthood. In Mormonism, a man's position as head of the home is embodied in his priesthood – this is what gives him divine authority in the family. Without the priesthood, if a black man's wife got sick and asked for a blessing, he would have to call a white member to come into his home and administer it for him. In effect, black men were not really even the heads of their own families.

Things stayed that way even when the South was burning in the mid-'60s. But in the seventies, something happened, and that something was Brazil.

The church had begun expanding aggressively into other countries, especially into South America. In Brazil, where slavery had been about ten times more widespread than in the US, the black population was so huge and so intricately integrated into society, it could not really be considered a minority. If the church were ever to gain a serious foothold there, it would have to revisit the doctrine of the Mark of Cain. So the prophet knelt down, prayed about it, and bingo: The Mark of Cain disappeared.

Some members couldn't accept it: If God's truth is eternal, he doesn't change his mind about things whenever a truth becomes unpleasant. Either the Mark of Cain was God's will or it wasn't. If it was, the church had now fallen away from the path of God. If it wasn't, it had never been led by God in the first place.

That reaction didn't surprise me. What surprised me was the other reaction: The great majority of members considered it for about five minutes and accepted the change with a sigh of relief.

I believe most Mormons were enormously grateful for the change. More than ten years after the civil rights movement had abolished the Jim Crow laws, the exclusion of blacks from the priesthood had become a deep embarrassment. Yet we were expected to defend it to outsiders. Part of being a Mormon was always defending an indefensible principle to non-members. And now, all of a sudden, the whole Mark of Cain thing was over. It was less a matter of God's eternal truth than it was of finally being able to hold our heads up high again.

That says a lot about Mormons. In theory, they are conservative and highly disapproving of lifestyles that deviate from the norm. In practice they are open to change. That's why I am convinced that the next couple of generation of Mormons will experience two big changes that have seemed impossible up to now:

- Homosexuality will be declared no longer a sin, and
- Women will be given the priesthood.

Though the church officially teaches that the homosexual act is a sin, views on the touchy subject among Mormons are surprisingly varied. They go from outright rejection to active Mormons who are gay and talk openly about their "problem," to angry activists who publish their experiences in books and blogs.

For example David Matheson, who went to therapy for years to cure himself of his homosexuality. Today (as of this writing) he says he is "not quite straight, but straight enough," and offers therapy to other members trying to "correct" their sexuality. Or Mitch Mayne, who is a practicing Mormon and openly gay. He protests against the prohibition of homosexuality and has said that he is still holding the option open to enter into a gay relationship some day – at the moment he lives in celibacy, which makes it possible to remain an active member and hold the priesthood (as with Catholics, in Mormonism the sin is not the homosexuality itself, but specifically the homosexual act). H. Stuart Matis repeatedly tried celibacy and therapy before one day writing a letter to his mother in which he described his life as a homosexual in the church as "…a life of constant torment, self-hatred and internalized homophobia" and appealed to the leadership of the church to rethink its anti-homosexual doctrine. Then he went to his local church and put a bullet through his head. Since then, gay Mormons occasionally hold "suicide watches" – meetings to remind members of the danger of suicide for their fellow gay members.

That kind of news has pushed the discussion about homosexuality into the open in recent years. In my time, in the '70s and the '80s, no one talked about it, but it was still in the back of everyone's heads.

I made up my mind about homosexuality when I was still a member, back in college in Hawaii. I was talking to a professor – a marine biologist, I think – not about homosexuality, but about hamsters. In passing, he mentioned something about the high percentage of homosexual hamsters.

"Wait," I said, "Hamsters are gay?"

"Sure," he said, "Most animal species have a substantial homosexual population."

Up to then, I had been taught that homosexuality was either due to a dominant mother or something men do because they spend too much time watching porn and are so debauched that normal sex just doesn't do it for them anymore. But … hamster porn? Hamster sex clubs?

I asked, "But where do they get the idea?"

I don't remember the professor's name, but I will never forget the weird look on his face when I asked that question.

Scientists began noticing homosexuality in animals in the 1980s and now have observed (depending on what reports you read) between 500 and 1500 different species that practice it, including bears, house cats, dolphins and even the mighty King of the Jungle, the lion. In many cases it's not clear whether it is "true homosexuality." Some animals, it appears, will simply have sex with anything that moves, but they return to the opposite sex to reproduce. Some may not be so much "homosexual" as simply uncontrollably horny. Since then, closer observation has led to proof of "true homosexuality" in at least some species: Some 10 percent of rams, for example, will mate exclusively with other rams and never touch a ewe, and in Hawaii, the monogamous Laysan albatross will choose a same-sex partner for life about 30 percent of the time – "lesbian" Laysans will often get themselves pregnant by males then return to their same-sex mates to raise their young, presumably leaving behind a string of broken-hearted heterosexual males in their wake.

That, for me, was the straw that broke the camel's back: If animals practice homosexuality, they don't do it because their society is debauched, they do it because God built it into their biology. Thus, homosexuality, too, was part of God's creation. I wasn't the only Mormon who figured that out, either: There are a lot of Mormons out there patiently waiting for the prophet to get on his knees and pray about the issue and receive the shocking news from God.

Feminists criticize the church as a patriarchy, which it is: Much like Catholicism, the priesthood in Mormonism is reserved for men and women are expected to make child-raising their priority and to respect their husbands as the head of the household.

The church resists change in the role of women fiercely, as if any such change threatened the very basis of Mormonism – the family. Even as women take on more and more power and leadership responsibility in the world, the church continues to pressure them to stay in the home, at least as long as the children are young. Even when it's clearly unrealistic: I remember in the '70s when the then-church president admonished women to stay at home, the reaction of many female members I knew was, "That sounds great, but how are we going to pay our bills?" About a day or two later, articles appeared in newspapers asking whether the church could even exist if women followed the president's advice: Somewhere close to half (if my memory serves me right) of the paid workforce in church administration were women.

The church's stubborn loyalty to outdated roles affects more than just a woman's career choices – it affects how they perceive themselves.

When I served a mission, the other new missionaries and I spent the first three months in the "Missionary Training Center" in Utah, where we learned what was expected of us as well as the rudiments of the new language. There, brother and sister missionaries ate and attended classes together, and I got to notice a few things about the few sister missionaries. None of them were very high on the adolescent totem pole of sexual attraction. One was a bit mousy, over-shy, with Coke-bottle glasses and a nervous little laugh; another was overweight and small, and when she ate, she covered her mouth, as if ashamed of eating. Not all of them lacked self-esteem, but most of them did.

They knew what the boys were thinking: "She's only on a mission because she can't get a boyfriend."

The church expects boys to go on a mission, but girls are encouraged to start thinking about founding a family while they are young. Girls who opt to go on a mission are automatically slapped with the unspoken, unacknowledged stigma that they could not get a man. And they feel it.

It doesn't matter that they are sacrificing one and half years of their young lives (half a year less than the boys) to serve God, spending their own money, willingly facing rejection and loneliness in the mission field, all because they believe, while the other girls sit around back home flirting and gossiping and making wedding plans. The most valiant and admirable women in the church are those who go on a mission – yet, the church rewards them by making them feel ashamed of themselves.

That is why the attitudes toward women in the church have to change, and I believe they will.

Having said that, it is only half the story.

If you asked me if the Mormon church was a patriarchy, based not on its structure but only on the women I knew, I would say that Mormonism is really a secret matriarchy.

I associate the word "patriarchy" with words like "exploitation" and "repression." It conjures up the image of women who are powerless and closed out of leadership circles, who work but do not enjoy the fruits of their labor to the same extent as their men do, and who obey their men in return for being placed on a pedestal and emptily worshipped as beautiful or morally superior so they have a false feeling of worth that is really just a consolation prize for living a life of dependence.

Then I look at my father and other Mormon men I have witnessed and I can't say I saw many who enjoyed any advantages of their patriarchy. In fact, I've often thought: If this is patriarchy, we're doing it wrong.

It starts with sexuality. In a patriarchy, the man enjoys the advantages of a double standard: He is allowed – with a wink – to live out his sexuality while the woman is expected to repress her own. Society shrugs its shoulders when a man has an affair, but when a woman goes astray, things get serious. Mormons don't wink. Males are held to the same strict standards as females are; boys are scared away from sex just as much as girls are, and when a marriage breaks up because of infidelity, the man is considered to blame more than the woman. No Mormon man enjoys a sexual advantage over women.

In theory, Mormon women are counseled to submit to the head of the household, and it's true that Mormons have a lot of respect for the family father, for his power of decision and for the hard work he does.

But when I look back at my father and other Mormon men, it's hard to imagine them ever actually doing something their wives disapproved of. I can't even imagine a Mormon man winning a fight with a Mormon woman, much less imagine him pushing his wife around or being waited on hand and foot by her. I'm sure there are Mormon men out there who put their foot down in an argument and yell, "I'm the head of the house and you will do as I say" – Mormon teachings certainly make that possible – but I doubt it happens often.

Mormon men do not spend their wages out drinking all night with their buddies – remember the Word of Wisdom? They do not go to whorehouses, they do not lose their money in Poker games – games of chance are forbidden – and because they are expected to take care of the family, most of their leisure time opportunities are devoted to family entertainment. Mormonism is constructed around the family, and the man is subject to the needs of the family. He hears that every Sunday in church: Your family comes first. Is your wife happy? Are you spending enough time with your children? I've never heard a sermon in church about the importance of working late, wielding power or being loyal to your male buddies.

Are men happy with the arrangement? I suspect they are. A Mormon man grows up knowing that wild parties, fast women and fast cars and all those macho comic book adventures he might have dreamt about are never going to be part of his life. But he also knows he will get the respect he deserves for all his hard work.

Are women happy with the arrangement?

In the '70s I was often puzzled when Mormon women vehemently defended their "traditional" roles and roundly rejected the "woman's lib" movement. I wondered why they never rebelled against the old-fashioned ideas about women that men in leadership positions propagated. After all, most women I knew worked – factually they already seemed emancipated to me. They must have known that emancipation was to their advantage.

BYU sociologists Cardell K. Jacobson and Tim B. Heaton determined in a study that while fewer Mormon women (only 25 percent) pursue full-time careers (the US average is 39 percent), in terms of part-time work it is the other way around: 23 percent of Mormon women work part-time, compared with the national average of 14 percent. That may indicate that Mormon women need the money like everyone else and are willing to work for it, but at the same time they want to be home when the kids get back from school.

If that is true, it means Mormon women tend to put their families first. That coincides with my experience: I believe Mormon women often see the church, including its outdated gender roles, as a means of creating and sustaining a wholesome, healthy, intact family – an ideal to which they are willing to sacrifice everything else.

That doesn't mean Mormon women accept repression or see themselves as the "weaker sex." On the contrary, the women I knew in the church were often stronger than the men. Growing up with Mormon women, I have always been surprised and a little puzzled when single woman outside the church complain that men "don't like strong women." Most women I knew, even if they never had the ambitions of a Hillary Clinton or a Bella Abzug, were strong. To me, strong women living in traditional roles were the norm.

It began on the prairie.

Hardship was a way of life for Mormon families in the early phases of the church, especially during and after the journey to Utah. It wasn't just the hardship of life in the desert or of the constant persecution they were subject to: Most converts were poor immigrants to begin with. They were used to fighting. A woman who leaves her homeland in Sweden, sails alone or with her family across the Atlantic then treks another 3,100 miles westward, often pushing a handcart, a shotgun always within reach, possibly even pregnant (again!), only to face the problem of coaxing corn to grow in soil that seldom saw rain, is not made of porcelain.

She is what Mormons call a "pioneer woman," and they still celebrate and emulate her today as the prototype Mormon female. Pioneer women are more than tradition, they are Mormon identity.

For me growing up, the prototype pioneer woman was an aunt of mine – I'll call her Aunt M.

We lived an ocean apart and I seldom saw her, but when I did, I never saw her sit down. Aunt M. ran around all day, organizing her 13 children, getting the older kids to dress the younger kids, getting the kids with free hands to peel potatoes and wash beans, taking children and neighbor kids to and from school and music lessons and the little league game, checking homework, making lists for her husband to do when he got home, harvesting the garden, running errands and doing chores – not to mention her jobs for the church, which, though she didn't hold the priesthood, were as time-consuming as the positions her husband held: organizing potluck night, chaperoning the church dance, preparing Sunday school lessons, attending leadership meetings for the church women's organization.

And smiling.

Bizarrely enough, that smile was a permanent feature of Aunt M.'s face, as was her persistently encouraging tone. I never heard her raise her voice, never heard a disparaging comment or complaint cross her lips. Anything less would have been for her, I believe, a personal failure. Much like a man might dream and strive his whole life to have his own successful business, her one ambition was to create and run a successful family, and nothing was going to stop her. Was she happy? I can't say. I'm sure there were times when she broke down, I'm sure she made mistakes and had regrets, and quite possibly many of her children feel now they were neglected by their overworked parents in their youth.

I don't know enough about Aunt M. and her family to say either way.

But I can say this: I have never met a stronger woman.

The second big prayer of my life came twelve years after the first.

I was 20, in Hawaii and the question this time was, *Should I go on a mission?*

If you're a missionary in almost any other church, you are a professional. You have studied theology for years, negotiated your terms, your expenses are paid and you take your wife and children with you. It is the first step in a theological career.

If you're a Mormon missionary, you have no intention whatsoever of having a church career. There are no careers in the Mormon church. You're dreaming of starting your own business or getting a good job at Google or becoming a scientist or, like me, finding a way to become a writer. All that is just beginning. You're enjoying the newfound freedoms of adulthood, exploring new ideas, making interesting new friends and learning about who you really are and your place in the world. And you've just met a girl.

That's the perfect time for the bishop to call you into his office and ask if you're ready to go on a voluntary, self-financed two-year mission to a place that would be revealed to you after you have already committed yourself.

But you knew what was coming. By that time you've talked to enough returned missionaries to know that a Mormon mission is best described in two words: Rejection and homesickness. For some reason, people don't appreciate being approached by complete strangers who want to talk to them about Jesus Christ.

And if there's a girl in your life before you leave, you know what's going to happen sometime in the next 24 months.

They call it a "Dear John letter."

A male missionary usually receives it about three to six months into his mission. It comes from the very girlfriend back home who had tearfully promised to wait the full two years. Now she's writing to tell him that she's met someone else. These letters don't start with "My Love," or "Honey Bunny," or "Hey Big Boy," they start a bit less passionately with something like "Dear John." Nothing brings a promising mission to a sudden stop like a Dear John letter. Stories of missionaries suddenly disappearing to get onto a plane to go back home to save their relationship are legendary. Others simply fall into despondency and refuse to get out of bed for weeks.

If you're nineteen years old and your bishop tells you the church would like to send you on a mission, you have a lot of serious thinking to do.

I thought about it all through my teens.

My older brothers and sisters had not gone, so I was my family's last chance to have a missionary in the family. Looking back, I realized how little pressure there was under the circumstances: My parents never tried to talk me into it. Though they would be happy if I went, I suspect it wasn't all that important to them – making sure I got a college education, for example, was clearly the priority.

As I began to plot out my future, I found I had three options:

1. Run off to New York to starve in an attic and become a writer;
2. Run off to Europe to study the Middle Ages, become a professor and write great novels on summer break;
3. Go on a mission and then return to either of the first two options with a two-year delay.

Going to Europe was the most attractive of the three, but how would I get there? The challenge was even more daunting than New York, which, for a boy from Hawaii, was scary enough. Then it occurred to me that I could combine Options 2 and 3: go on a mission in Europe.

This is the thing about going on a mission: You do not choose our destination. The church sends you where you are most needed. But there was a way around that: If you could speak a language besides English, the church would probably send you to a place where that language was spoken.

Kailua High School offered, if I recall correctly, three or four foreign languages, including Japanese, Spanish and German. Japan was clearly not Europe and I didn't want to get sent to South America, so I picked German. I knew nothing about Germany at the time and had no natural inclination to visit the place, but it could get me to Europe, so I checked the box.

It was a confusing and torturous time for me. On the one hand, the German language was so horribly difficult and apparently without any inner logic whatsoever, that sitting through class was physically painful. I remember the dread and despair each morning upon entering the classroom, knowing full well I was willingly inflicting yet another hour of failure and defeat upon myself.

There was only one compensation: The teacher was the sexiest woman in school. I managed to get myself through three years of straight Ds by sitting there every day and doing little more than dreaming about her the entire hour.

It paid off.

The day I learned where I would go for my mission was sunny and warm and there was salt in the air, a typical day for Hawaii. I had just returned home from work, I grabbed a handful of letters from the mailbox and shed my thongs (which is what we called flip-flops in Hawaii back then) outside the front door. The house was empty. Sand crunched underfoot while I walked from room to room opening the windows to let a little air in.

One of the letters was addressed to me. It was from Salt Lake City, Utah.

Time stood still. I could hear myself breathe. The cat was watching me from the living room table. This was the moment I had been waiting for.

I ripped open the letter and scanned past the blah blah of the opening paragraphs until I found the important part: "... Düsseldorf, Germany."

I was more than a year behind most other missionaries. After high school I had talked my parents into letting me stay at home for a year so I could write my first novel. For over a year I thought about it and still couldn't decide: My novel ... my grand career as a brilliant writer ... two years getting jeered at on the streets ... I'd been wondering whether to go on a mission or not since I hit puberty and still didn't know.

So I did what every Mormon does who faces a major decision: I knelt down and prayed.

I remember that prayer well. Where I knelt in my room, the lateness of the hour, the silence in the rest of the house. The question I asked.

It wasn't, "Should I go on a mission?" This was not about that, not directly. That decision was dependent on the larger question of whether the church was true. If the church was true, then God really wanted me to go on a mission. Nothing else was relevant. It was the same question I asked when I was eight, but as an adult you can't base your life on decisions you made when you were a kid. The question whether the church was true or not was one that had to be asked again and again. It's a living, evolving question.

I knelt down and refused to get up until I knew.

It wasn't easy. It's not normal to concentrate on a single thought over a long period of time. My mind drifted in and out, to my plans, to the novel I was working on and which would make me famous ... stop that, I am trying to talk to God here, I am asking God a question and I expect an answer ... oh, but I am going to miss the next Steven Spielberg movie. I wasn't very much into girls yet, but I was into movies, and Hollywood was in the midst of its *Jaws-Star Wars-Close Encounters-Apocalypse Now*-heyday and I didn't want to miss a moment, but you can't go to movies on a mission, they only distract you from the work, I would have to leave all that behind (indeed, one of the first questions put to me when I got back two years later was, "Wait, you're telling me you don't know who Indiana Jones is?"), okay stop that, you're trying to talk to God, concentrate.

Then it came. It was just there, that warm feeling of conviction, it flooded through me and settled into the depth of my belly.

Yes, the church was true.

When I got up, I saw that I had been on my knees for an hour.

The next morning I announced to my parents that I was going on a mission.

When I think back on those two years, I think of one sentence.

A missionary in a foreign country spends a lot of time studying the language. I started out very weak and it took me about half a year of speaking and studying German every day before I could hold a halting conversation. Ironically, it was largely unnecessary. With very few exceptions, missionaries in Germany need only one sentence – and it's not even a whole sentence:

Guten Tag, wir kommen von der Kirche Jesu Christi der Heiligen der Letzten Tage und möchten...

"Good day, we come from the Church of Jesus Christ of Latter-Day Saints and would like to..."

That's when the door slams.

For a long time I thought the Germans had as much trouble with their language as I did, because I only ever heard two words:

Keine Zeit. "No time."

I remember the first time my more experienced companion and I actually got in a door and sat down to talk about the gospel with a middle-aged woman who owned an iguana in a terrarium in the little town of Remscheid.

I had already been in Germany a couple of months and was eager to start teaching, but language-wise I was just beginning to come out of a fuzzy haze of not understanding what was going on around me. I could ask for help buying food in a supermarket and hold a rudimentary conversation with the neighbors about the weather ("It is raining!" "The sun is shining!"). And I had the "lessons" more or less memorized.

Ah, the lessons:

Missionaries are not theologians. They are just normal kids who may or may not have paid attention in Sunday school. In order to even make it possible for us to "teach the gospel," the church devised a series of "lessons" about the history and teachings of the church, written to function not only as information but also as a sales pitch, which missionaries memorize and repeat, using a little flip chart of visual aids. Of course, anything that goes beyond that – questions, objections, contradictory scriptures and just general conversation – the missionaries have to deal with on their own.

A missionary's most powerful tool is his "testimony" – his personal story of finding the church, reading the Book of Mormon, praying to God and asking if the church is true and receiving an answer.

I cannot exaggerate how important the concept of the "testimony" is in Mormon life in general. All Mormons have one, and all Mormons are expected to share it with others regularly. One Sunday a month is dedicated to bearing your testimony – instead of sermons, the time is given over to the members, who, much as in a support group, at first hesitate then step up to the pulpit and share with the congregation something about their lives and how God helped them. They generally close by bearing their testimony. Though a testimony is highly personal, members are used to routinely talking about it, baring their souls without flinching, even to complete strangers. That influences how members deal with each other – it creates a basic atmosphere of sincerity. Only when I left the church did I notice that life outside is generally colder, and sincerity, as a personal gift one person gives to another, is relatively rare.

In my case, my testimony was the story of my two big prayers. A testimony is a very personal story, and if you tell it sincerely, it can be very emotional and powerful. In addition to the lessons, I could give my testimony in German. I just couldn't hold a normal conversation.

That day I didn't have a good grasp on all the details of the conversation going on in front of me, but I understood enough that I thought I could contribute something. We were sitting in the woman's cozy living room and she had even brought out tea and cookies. But there was a bitter look on her face and a strident tone in her voice, and I knew why. We were talking about the Mormon concept of the eternal family – Mormons believe you marry for eternity and will be together with your family and loved ones in the afterlife. That's when she mentioned her husband, who was no longer with her. It had happened about a year ago, that's how long she'd been a widow, and it had made her bitter, you could tell.

This was my chance. In what was not perfect but certainly understandable German, I told her, "Don't you want to be with him again for all eternity?"

That's when things blew up. Without warning, she went into a hostile rant that didn't seem to want to end, and my companion had his hands full just getting us out of there. The only sentence I understood in the landslide of invectives and exclamation marks was something about "shooting to the moon." When we were finally out on the street again, my annoyed but amused companion explained what *zum Mond schiessen* meant:

She hated her husband so much she wanted to shoot him to the moon and even that was not far enough away.

I had apparently misunderstood the part about her being a widow: Her husband had not died, he had simply left her for a younger woman.

I went back to studying.

Every once in a while, someone would call the cops.

It usually happened the day after certain kinds of shows ran on public TV – documentaries that warned against dangerous cults. These documentaries made things interesting for us, but unfortunately, since we were not allowed to watch TV, we never knew in advance.

Once in Dortmund, my companion and I were coming out of an apartment block when we glanced back at the building we had gone through about fifteen minutes before. Five cop cars were parked outside. It looked like they were searching the building. Another man was standing nearby, so we asked him if he knew what was going on. He didn't know either. Then I asked him if he had seen anything on TV the night before about dangerous cults (my German was much better by then). He seemed to recall there was some kind of documentary. My companion and I knew what the commotion was all about.

In Germany, church is not separated from state as it is in America and some other countries. The Catholic and Lutheran churches give religion classes in public schools and their representatives sit on the supervisory boards of the state-financed public broadcasters. To make good with the churches, the public channels regularly run documentaries about dangerous cults, which are generally defined as any church that competes with the Catholics and Lutherans.

We walked back and told the officers that we might be the two suspicious characters they were looking for. After a bit of confused communication, we were taken inside, where the officer in charge was talking to residents in the stairwell. He confirmed that someone had called the police about members of a dangerous cult trying to kidnap children. Every once in a while, an old woman would appear on the stairs above and mutter something, pointing at us, then quickly scuttle away – we guessed she was the one who had been watching TV the night before. We showed him our IDs and government-issued missionary licenses and explained what we were doing, but the cop was still suspicious. He rummaged through our backpacks, noting the number of Books of Mormon we were vainly trying to give away, and our binder with visual aids.

That's when he found our door-to-door book.

To keep track of where we had and hadn't been, we kept a small notebook with all the addresses of the houses we had already visited. Here's how it worked: When you got to an apartment building, you drew a little grid that corresponded to the battery of doorbells. It was usually about four or five rows high and three or four columns across. When we rang a doorbell and someone said *"Keine Zeit,"* we placed an X in the corresponding box so we wouldn't ring there again when we swept through the street a second time a few weeks later. If no one answered, we left the box open.

So we were carrying around a little booklet with charts of every apartment building in the neighborhood with some of the apartments marked with an X.

The officer in charge found this very intriguing.

We explained it to him, but he remained unconvinced and continued paging through it to the very end. In the back, we had scribbled a handful of motivational sayings that we would sometimes refer to when the rejection got too oppressive. "Whatever the mind of man can conceive and believe, it can achieve," was one saying, and there were lots of quotes from the motivational speaker Zig Ziglar, like "You were designed for accomplishment, engineered for success, and endowed with the seeds of greatness," things like that.

And this:

You can't always get what you want,
but if you try sometimes,
well you just might find,
you get what you need.

The officer in charge wasn't very good at English, so he asked us to translate this quote. Which I did. He still didn't get it. So I sang it to him – twice: "But if you try sometimes – *bum bum bum* – you just might find – *bum bum bum* – you get what you ne-eed! (oooh baby!)"

When he still didn't get it, his second-in-command leaned over and whispered into his ear: "Rolling Stones."

Without flinching, he slowly closed the book and gave it back to us and said he would let us go this time with a warning. I had the distinct impression this wasn't what he had become a cop for.

I've thought a lot about that funny little encounter and others like it.

They tell you in school that separation of church and state is necessary for democracy, but it is not true. Germany does not separate church and state, yet German democracy functions very well.

The German government collects a so-called "church tax" that all Catholics and Lutherans in the country have to pay alongside their state taxes. Besides teaching religion class in schools and sitting on the boards that supervise state-financed TV and radio broadcasters, representatives of the Catholics and Lutheran churches also monitor all the state-run arts organizations, including the agencies that fund film production.

This has a strong influence on how Germans think: They are told again and again, starting in school, that the only legitimate Christian religions are the Lutherans and Catholics. Other churches are allowed, of course, but anyone adhering to a faith other than Lutheranism or Catholicism is viewed with extreme suspicion.

The advantage to the system is that it keeps a lid on the crazies. There are far fewer weird religions and cults in Germany than in America. The disadvantage is that religion becomes stagnant. German churches are empty, and religious thought has stagnated: The last interesting religious idea to come out of Germany was Martin Luther.

Every once in a while, church leaders in America moan and groan that the separation of church and state is too strict – they want to display the Ten Commandments in courthouses or teach "Intelligent Design" in schools. They should take a look at Germany.

It is no coincidence that "new" religions, including the Mormons, can take root and flourish in America, but seldom in many other countries: It's because the government doesn't protect or support any one denomination. Once the state takes over, religion becomes stagnant. Whenever I hear a Southern Baptist or a Methodist or even a Mormon complaining that the state won't give them access to children in schools, I want to shake them and say: "The only reason your church exists today is because of the laws you are complaining about now."

Maybe it's true that if you try hard enough, you get what you need. I only made one convert in my two years in Germany, but that convert led to the most intensely beautiful spiritual experience of my life.

I will call her A. I met her in Krefeld.

My companion and I did not find her going door to door, but by recommendation. A church member had given us the name and address of her mother, who was curious. When we showed up for our appointment, it quickly became apparent that the mother was not so much interested as polite, but we went through the motions anyway. Somewhere toward the middle of the lesson, a young girl walked into the room, sat down and began listening.

A. was pretty, friendly and had a serious vibe about her, but gave no indication that she was listening. Surprisingly, when the lesson was over and the mother hemmed and hawed about us returning another time, A. said she wanted to learn more.

It progressed quickly from there. In a series of chaperoned visits, we taught her the lessons, persuaded her to attend church meetings and read the Book of Mormon, and when we asked her if she had prayed about whether the church was true or not and wanted to be baptized, she said yes. Miraculously, her mother – A. was still 16 – gave permission.

The life of a missionary is blazing hot and freezing cold, a constant white-knuckled rebound between never-ending rejection and cheerful, pie-in-the-sky motivational speeches from our mission president, whose job was not only to organize us, but to keep us going against relentless resistance. Sometimes the rousing "You can do it, you just have to want it" sermons we heard over and over and needed like an addict needs his drug were as punishing as the rejection. But I kept going. I didn't know I had the strength to keep going, but surprisingly, I did. I wanted it. I wanted it badly. I wanted at least one baptism, and I finally got it.

This is what being a missionary is about – maybe it's what being a Mormon, even a being a human being is about: 99 percent hardship, and just when you think it will never come, 1 percent reward. You lose faith, you can't avoid losing faith, but still, one day the success comes. No matter how long it takes, if you just keep holding on for dear life, it comes.

In the days before the scheduled baptism I was high with a feverish, unreal exuberance and at the same time deeply paranoid that this success would be snatched from me at the last minute. In those days I prayed like never before.

The day of the baptism, as we drove from Krefeld to Düsseldorf, where the church had a baptismal font, we had to keep telling ourselves along the way, like a mantra, "She'll come, she'll come." When we saw her standing there, it was like a miracle.

As I had done with my father years before, I changed into white and entered the baptismal room, where she was waiting for me, also dressed in white. Together we descended the steps into the lukewarm water, I placed my left hand on the small of her back and raised my right, spoke the short prayer and lowered her backward into the water. The surface closed around her head and calmed a little, and I took a good look to make sure every hair was submerged, then I pulled her out again.

Mormons believe the Holy Ghost is present at baptisms and testifies in the hearts of the participants that what they are doing is right. He was there that day. I felt an almost ecstatic light vibrate within and around me. The room appeared brighter, the world was suddenly weightless and so was I, as if I were breathing divine air that made me light-headed and burned inside. I felt God there with us that day.

My story with A. did not end with her baptism.

I was too stupid to notice it, but she was interested in more than just the church. Shortly after the baptism, I was transferred to Oberhausen, which was to become the last stop on my mission. There, she visited me twice – along with a group of other young people from the church in Krefeld, a kind of unofficial chaperone, as it was forbidden for missionaries to meet with young women alone. We were awkward together. I didn't know how to act, neither did she. We didn't know each other, we weren't actually friends, we were just bound together by this one experience. That connection was so intense I knew it would last a lifetime, I just didn't know what to do with it. There is no such thing as a "baptizer/baptizee" relationship. I just knew I was glad to see her, and she was happy to see me. Once, when it was time for them to leave, I wondered if she wasn't fighting back tears.

A few months later, as I was preparing to end my two-year stint and return home, I realized I didn't want to leave her. I didn't dare use the word "love," even to myself, but I knew I didn't want her to fade away and become just another memory.

The day I was to take the train to Düsseldorf, from where I would travel to Frankfurt and get on a plane, I made one of the boldest decisions of my life. I was going to break the rules.

It sounds silly today, but I was a good missionary and to me breaking any rule – most especially a rule like this – was a grave act of disobedience. Of the many instructions we received as we prepared to return home, the most important was to travel directly to Düsseldorf, not to take any detours, neither to see the sights nor to meet anyone. Especially not to meet anyone. Suddenly that rule seemed arbitrary. I mean, what's the difference? For the first time I was consciously going to disobey the mission president.

I got on the train to Krefeld. I arrived early in the morning, but I only had less than an hour before I needed to get on my connecting train. She had her own attic room above her mother's apartment. I knocked, and through the door she asked who it was. I tried to make a joke of it, disguise my voice, but I didn't do it well. She'd known I was leaving Germany today. She was still in pajamas, and I think she might have been crying.

Now she smiled, nervous. Neither of us knew what to do. I was very aware of protocol, however, and of the fact that being alone with a young woman in pajamas presented the Devil with his last chance to destroy my mission. I asked if we could talk – in her mom's kitchen.

We didn't have much to say. We mainly sat there, aware that the clock was ticking. Finally I gathered up all my courage and forced myself to say: *"Ich glaube, ich habe Gefühle für Sie."*

I think I have feelings for you.

I even used the formal *Sie*. German has two ways of saying "you" – to your mother, God and the one you love, you use the intimate *Du* ("thou"). For strangers, the police and your boss, you use the more formal *Sie* ("you"). One of the many rules imposed on missionaries to keep them from getting too close to young women was that they are never to use the intimate *Du*. Most missionaries don't even bother to learn *Du*.

Sitting there with the young woman I was in love with, I addressed her formally, as a missionary should. I couldn't even bring myself to use the word "love." So all I said was that I had feelings for her.

She replied that she had feelings for me too.

I had done what I had come to do and it was time to go. We shook hands and I left to catch the train.

CHAPTER 3

Americans in Heaven

IT'S ALL TRUE: ALL THE RUMORS YOU'VE HEARD ABOUT how weird, crazy, absolutely whacko Mormons are. Mormonism really is the weirdest denomination in all of Christianity.

It's only when you take a closer look that all the weirdness makes sense.

The first thing you notice when trying to figure out Mormonism is Joseph Smith's uniquely pragmatic approach to theology.

When faced with a knotty question like transubstantiation – whether the wafer and wine "in substance" turn into the flesh and blood of Christ it your mouth – Europeans will produce reams of convoluted theological argument. Mormons won't even entertain the notion: "Are you nuts? That's cannibalism. You shouldn't even have to ask that question. Of course it's only symbolic."

Most theological principles of Mormonism are likewise shored up by simple common sense, including the idea that God speaks to prophets on earth today.

The Bible is full of prophets – they are constantly talking to God's chosen people and giving them commandments, visions and admonitions. So why not now? Are we so much wiser than in olden days that we no longer need his exhortations? Did God say all he wanted to say in the Bible and has nothing to add about the problems facing us today? Did he just plain give up on us?

Joseph Smith saw that the simplest answer is sometimes the best: God still talks, we just stopped listening. Thus, each president of the church is at the same time a prophet.

Or hell.

If God is a God of love, how can he throw his own children into everlasting damnation? Joseph Smith saw this contradiction and did away with hell altogether. In its place, he divided heaven into "three degrees of glory:" The "celestial," the "terrestrial" and the "telestial" kingdoms. The most faithful of God's children will be sent to the highest degree of heaven, the worst of us will end up in the lowest. But even that, Smith said, is so beautiful, if we on earth ever caught a glimpse of it, we would immediately commit suicide just to get there.

Or the Trinity.

The question of the Trinity is one of the most difficult problems in Christian theology: there is only one God, but at the same time there are three – God the Father, Jesus Christ and the Holy Ghost. Only, they aren't really three gods at all, they are three gods in one, because there is only one God, but at the same time there are three of them... Try reading the Wikipedia entry on the Trinity sometime – it's excruciating. I suspect that some time in the past someone had a silly idea, but no one wanted to tell him it was silly, so they went along with it and ended up spending the next centuries trying to explain something that was unexplainable. By now they've dug themselves in too deep ever to admit it was all just one big misunderstanding.

Joseph Smith was never overawed by ancient wise men talking nonsense. When he wrote the final versions of his "First Vision," he was careful to make clear that the two personages who appeared to him were distinctly separate beings – God the Father and Jesus Christ, his son. Two independent beings, not two-in-one. Jesus is not an "expression" of God, nor is he God in some other way – only God is God; Jesus is his son.

Together with the Holy Ghost, who is also a separate and independent being, but without a physical body, the three of them form a kind of three-person leadership committee with separate tasks: God is our father and Creator; Jesus, as his first-born son, took upon himself the sacrifice that redeemed us in God's eyes, and the Holy Ghost mediates spiritually between God and us. (The Trinity problem, by the way, is the reason some churches won't recognize Mormonism as a Christian faith. They claim you can't be Christian unless you believe Jesus was actually God in disguise. Mormons don't mind – they don't take people seriously who can't explain their own beliefs, anyway.)

With all the intellectual energy that Christianity puts into inventing hugely complicated answers to simple questions, it has always astounded me that most churches have never tried to definitively answer the one question that calls into doubt everything Christianity claims to be:

If God loves all mankind and wants us all to know his truth and return to him, why does he inform so few of us about it?

Statistically speaking, very few people in the world today and throughout history have ever heard of Jesus Christ. How many people growing up in Tibet, in India or Indonesia, in Africa or China over the last 2000 years had the chance to "accept Christ?" Not many. According to accepted Christian teaching, these people – the majority of the human race – will not have a chance to return to God.

All Christian churches are founded on the principle that to return to God, you have to wash yourself free of sin by accepting Jesus's sacrifice. That's what Jesus meant when he said, "Except that a man be born of water and of the Spirit, he cannot enter into the kingdom of God" (John 3:5). This simple statement, referring to baptism as a symbolic rebirth, is what justifies any Christian church. If Jesus had said, "To get to heaven you have to be a good person," churches as institutions would not be necessary. Unfortunately, he didn't say that – he said you need the rite of baptism, and that rite is provided by an institution invested with the authority from God to perform it.

Modern Christianity pretends to be all-inclusive, and we like to portray God as loving all his children, but the dirty truth is that the necessity of baptism implicitly condemns everyone to hell who died without the chance. That doesn't sound like something a loving God would do. Yet, no traditional Christian church I know has ever seriously addressed that problem.

Joseph Smith took the question seriously and came up with an answer: Baptism by proxy.

If you're a Mormon, once or twice a year you spend half a day in the temple, usually on a Saturday, where you dress in white, step into the warm water of the baptismal font and let a priesthood-holder dunk you beneath the surface while reading a name that neither of you has heard before, something like, "Abner MacKenzie, I baptize you in the name of the Father, the Son and the Holy Ghost." When you come out of the water, the process is repeated, this time with a different name, until you have been baptized in the name of dozens of people you will never meet because they are dead.

The theory behind it is that the dead are watching from the so-called "spirit world," where we all patiently await the Second Coming, resurrection and judgment. In that limbo-like place, they have had the chance to talk to spirit missionaries (yes, there will be Mormon missionaries in the spirit world) about the gospel of Christ and now must make a decision: Will they accept the proxy baptism that took place in their name on earth? The baptism itself – which has to be performed on earth, as it is a physical act – takes place whether they like it or not, but it only becomes valid if the deceased accept it. There's even a mysterious verse in the Bible that implies that the original church had a similar practice. Paul writes: "Else what shall they do which are baptized for the dead, if the dead rise not at all? Why are they then baptized for the dead?" (1 Corinthians 15:29).

While most churches shrug their shoulders at the billions of people who died without having a chance to be baptized, the Mormon church is slowly but surely, name for name, baptizing them all.

To find the names of the unbaptized dead, they spend an enormous amount of time, energy and money on genealogical research – tracking down as many names as possible, like detectives, starting with their own ancestors. The church runs the largest databank for genealogical research in the world, the heart of which is the eight-million-dollar Family History Library in Salt Lake City, which holds some four million rolls of microfilmed records from 110 countries estimated to contain some two billion names, and makes that data open to non-Mormons as well. Though the church does not say how many people it has already baptized by proxy, estimates run somewhere near 100 million, and rumor has it that even such famous names as the Founding Fathers, Stalin and Hitler and a number of Popes have been baptized in this way, which goes to show that Mormons believe there is a place in heaven even for Catholics. (When you ask Mormons about the billions of names in history that went unrecorded and that will never turn up in any genealogical research, they say they have trust that God will provide a way, perhaps after the Second Coming.)

Looking back today, I realize how rare it is for so many people to be so dedicated to a purpose that has no material value in this world whatsoever. They don't get paid for it and the church only loses money on it. No third party profits from it, either – when you give to a charity or do volunteer work, you know more or less where the money is going, you can see the results. You can't see the results of your genealogical work. It is entirely idealistic – it is an investment in people you do not know, who are dead, without expecting any visible result at all.

Speaking of the temple:

Mormons attend Sunday services (as well as a string of weekday activities) in a church like everyone else, but baptisms for the dead and other sacred rites are reserved for the 150 or so temples that they operate worldwide. While anyone can enter a church, to get into a temple you have to be found "worthy" in a private interview with your bishop, which means you have to convince him that you are currently keeping the church's commandments.

On the one hand, Mormon temples are Joseph Smith's practical answer to the question, "If the ancient Hebrews had temples, why don't modern Christians?" At the same time, they are the centerpiece of the Mormon love for family.

Baptism for the dead is performed primarily for the ancestors of Mormons: It is an attempt to keep as much of the family as possible together in heaven, including the extended family. That is also the purpose of "eternal marriage" and "sealing." A marriage performed in a temple is believed to be valid even after death, for all eternity, and children who are "sealed" to their parents in the temple will remain part of that family for eternity as well. Mormons envision not only themselves alive and well in the afterlife, they see their entire happy families there with them.

Of course, you can't get to heaven unless you obey God's commandments. So in the temple, individual Mormons perform a rite in which they renew their covenant with God – the same covenant they made at baptism, but this time the rite is more intense.

Temple initiates are clothed in special "garments" (called "magic underwear" by detractors), which reach from the shoulders to the knees and carry four Masonic-like symbols sewn into the fabric (over the heart, over one knee, etc.) that remind Mormons of various aspects of their temple vows (Smith based many of the secret clothing, rites and handshakes for the temple from

Freemasonry, of which he was a member most of his life). Temple-goers are expected to wear their garments underneath their clothes day and night for the rest of their lives as a sign of devotion to God and as a reminder of their covenant with him (not in the shower or at the beach, of course, and – I would assume for most Mormons – not during sex).

"Magic underwear" demands the same kind of idealism that baptism for the dead requires:

Garments are not like wearing a cross around your neck or even a kippah: They cover nearly all your body. What's more, your friends know you're wearing them and are probably looking at you funny right now. You have to be pretty dedicated to your faith to wear them. There is something archaic about that kind of devotion. Garments put me in mind of ancient religions, like the Sikhs, who do not cut their hair, always wear a turban and, in some variations, carry a ceremonial dagger at all times. That level of dedication is something we've lost in modern life, where we expect to enjoy lots of privileges while doing very little to earn them. Being a Mormon demands more of you than any other Christian church I know.

The temple experience is more than just renewing vows, however – it is where Mormons are initiated into Joseph Smith's uniquely American and surprisingly democratic cosmology.

To understand what is democratic about the Mormon church (which, after all, doesn't vote for its leaders), you have to understand what Mormons mean when they say God is our "Father in Heaven." It's a phrase we're all used to hearing, but we never think about it. Why "father?" Why not just call him "Our God and Creator" and leave it at that?

Joseph Smith must have asked himself that and came up with a deceptively simple answer: We call God our "Father in Heaven" because he is our father. Literally: God not only created us, he conceived us.

This is how it works:

Before we were born on earth to our physical parents, we all existed in heaven as spirits (we were an extremely large family). We did not have physical bodies, but we were still intelligent, self-reflective individuals – God was our father and his wife was our mother (yes, Mormons believe God has a wife – how else can you produce children?). It is never explained in detail how God's physical body conceived of spirit children, but the important idea comes across clearly: As his spiritual children, we carry God's DNA. (Quite a number of details about the pre-existence are subject to dispute among Mormon theologians, and the interesting question of why we don't know more about our Mother in Heaven has, unfortunately, never been addressed in depth by the prophets.)

I do not imagine life in the "pre-existence," as Mormons call it, to have been particularly interesting. With no major changes or challenges confronting us and with God watching us constantly, I suspect spirit life was fairly predictable. Apparently, God felt the same way.

To mix things up, he created Earth and announced a plan to send us all there, where we would be born anew as physical entities with limited life spans, limited possibilities, limited consciousness, with no memory of our pre-existence and most importantly, no contact with God. And oh yes: subject to pain and suffering.

On earth we would know – for the first time – sickness and death; conflict, disappointment and unhappiness. We would have to struggle just to live, much less live a life with any kind of satisfaction. Our lives would be subject to inequality and hatred, uncontrollable physical desires, earthquakes and disease and wildly improbable events of chance.

And most of us would react to hardship in a predictably despicable way. In heaven, with God watching us, we would never dare commit any morally compromising act. But on earth, bad behavior would often appear the only reasonable solution to the challenges that face us. Our former brothers and sisters, whom we knew in heaven as pretty nice people, would begin acting crazy. They would instigate wars and bloodshed, turn brutal and exploitive, stab each other in the backs just to pursue silly things like money, power, sex and fame, which were unknown to us in the pre-existence. And not only our former brothers and sisters would do things they'd never do under God's watchful eye – we would too.

For the first time, we would be wholly alone in our decisions.

To makes matters worse, how we acted on earth would determine where we ended up in eternity.

When our earthly bodies died and we returned to God, we would face judgment. (You didn't think a truly Protestant church would ever forget about the judgment part, did you?) Those who – in their earth lives – proved themselves unworthy of their divine inheritance would not be allowed back into God's presence. Only those who proved they were truly God's children would be allowed to live with him in the "celestial" kingdom.

If you think about that, it's actually quite disturbing: God was asking us to go through a kind of test on earth without knowing what we were being tested for, and the outcome would determine our lives in all eternity. Not only that, he obviously didn't expect the majority of us to pass the test.

When God told us the full extent of his plan, some of us got worried. And when he put it to a vote, about a third of us voted against.

Instead of accepting the majority decision, the third who lost, rebelled. Led by one of our brothers said to be the brightest among us – Lucifer – the nay-faction tried to force God to abandon the plan. The rebellion didn't work. God cast them out, damning them to remain spirits forever, never to receive physical bodies, never to progress into the next stage of life and never to return to his presence.

Joseph Smith didn't invent the rebellion in heaven: The idea that demons or devils are fallen angels is as old as the Bible. Luke 10:18 mentions: "I saw Satan fall like lightning from heaven," and the Book of Revelations describes a "War in Heaven." And of course there's that *ur*-Protestant John Milton, who took all those clues and told the story of Lucifer's rebellion against God in *Paradise Lost*.

Mormons take the idea that we are all children of God to its ultimate conclusion: They don't merely want to return to God the Father and live with him as his children, they want to become like him. Yes, you read correctly: Mormons want to become Gods.

Most Christian churches use the term "Children of God," but they seldom think about the implications. Part of the definition of "child" is the idea that you will eventually grow up to be like Mom and Dad. You may not become a television repair man if your father repairs televisions, but you will follow the general trajectory of his life: You will have some other career, you will fall in love and found a family, you will raise your children just as your parents did and watch as they grow up. And they will do the same.

No parent would ever expect their children to remain children and live all their lives at home. The family dog does that – when a puppy "grows up," it doesn't move out, find a job and buy a pet of its own. It remains the family dog all its life. But children are expected to become adults in the same way their parents did.

If we on earth have divine parentage, that means we, too, will eventually grow up to be like our Father in Heaven. If father is a god, we can also develop into gods.

This is how it works: If you are obedient, go to the temple and remain worthy, after death you will enter into the highest of the three kingdoms, where you will be given the opportunity to give birth to spirit children. For children to develop further, you will send them to live on a planet you have created for them, where they will experience a physical, mortal life and learn the valuable lessons that are only possible there. When your children return to you, you will give them the opportunity to develop in the same way you did, by becoming gods themselves and creating worlds for their children.

That implies something about God's past as well: He, too, must have been a spirit child at one point, with a divine father who sent him to live a mortal life on a planet somewhere, just as we are doing now. Joseph Smith said, "God Himself was once as we are now." Later, another church president developed the idea further: "As man now is, God once was; as God now is, man may be."

Joseph Smith was not the first to have the idea: Some Orthodox and early Christian mystics kicked around a similar idea for a while, called "theosis" or "deification," but Europe quickly stamped out that kind of talk and today the Mormon vision of eternity is so wholly different from everything else, people raised in traditional Christianity think of Mormons as megalomaniacs. The feeling is mutual: Mormons tend to think of traditional Christians as subservient and unimaginative.

European Christianity was born in feudalism and it is still informed by feudal ideas. European Christians think of God as sitting upon a throne wearing a crown: God as a divine monarch. Think about that. In feudalism, a monarch can never become a serf because he was born to be a monarch. Likewise, his serfs are born into their subservient positions and cannot rise above. Thus it is with the European God: He was always God, he did not earn that position; likewise, his creations, mankind, will forever remain subservient to him and can never rise above their stations.

Americans rejected feudalism because they saw no reason why a peasant could not eventually become as rich and powerful as a king. Joseph Smith simply applied American meritocracy to

Christianity and said: If I am God's child, there's no reason why I can't grow up to become like him.

The doctrine of "eternal progression" – the idea that we were born before earth life and can become gods after – is the greatest and most courageous idea in Christianity since Luther.

We all know people who complain – in more or less those words – "Hey, I never asked to be born." You will never hear that from a Mormon. Church members believe that everyone on earth voted, in the pre-existence, to come here. We didn't know where or when we would be sent to earth; we had no say in whether we would be born into a rich or poor family. We knew the risks. Yet, we said: "Yes, I want to go."

That's courage.

When you grow up believing that, it affects you. You learn from the start that you are here of your own free will, that you were brave to take that primal risk, that you have a purpose here. Mormon children grow up believing they are on Earth because they wanted to be here and Mormon parents teach their children, long before they are old enough to face the moral dilemmas of adult life, that they are, deep in the core of their being, courageous individuals, and have already proven it.

Traditional European Christianity imagines earth life as something to be suffered, overcome and forgotten, like a trauma. That says a lot about how they see Creation: as a horrible mistake that needs correcting, a prison to escape from.

Mormonism defines Creation as something difficult but beautiful, a challenge that will make us stronger, as a meaningful phase in our development that we will build upon later. Mormons regularly compare earth life to leaving home for school or otherwise to live on your own.

When I look back on my first years on my own, I realize now how naïve I was. I thought I had it all figured out. I thought I could conquer any challenge and maybe even change the world. What really happened was that I just got by, and today, looking back, I realize that I was never nearly as heroic, as morally just, or as admirable as I imagined I would be. Life on my own was similar to what Michelangelo supposedly said about his art: "Every block of stone has a statue inside it and it is the task of the sculptor to discover it." The statue I found inside the block of stone wasn't the one I expected. But at least I'm no longer just a block of stone.

Getting whittled down from a block of stone to a work of art – even if it's not quite the work of art you had ordered – that's earth life according to Mormonism.

And if life is like a school, then death is graduation.

Here on earth, when we complete our education, we enter a new phase full of new responsibilities and challenges. Most importantly, this new phase requires that we use the knowledge and skills we acquired in school: If we studied business management, we get a job in which we can apply what we learned. Likewise, the experience of earth life gives us skills and experiences we will later need to meet the challenges of being gods.

Traditional Christians don't see it like that: Nothing we learn on earth is useful in our lives in eternity. As far as I can tell, European Christian theology sees us all, in the afterlife, gathering at God's feet and happily singing his praises for all eternity. You don't need to go to college for that.

Think about that. To eternally sing praises to God, all you need is a voice. You don't need to have gone through any of the things we experience here on earth – the love and loss, the longing and disappointment, the striving, success and failure, the happiness and grief, the development of our moral personalities. In the European version of Christianity, the experience of earth life has no lasting consequences other than to determine whether we will go to heaven or hell.

So you have Einstein, the Beatles, Michelangelo, da Vinci, Churchill and Gandhi and all kinds of great human beings doing all sorts of great things here on earth – but once they get to heaven, someone sticks a lyre in their hands and tells them to start singing. On earth they showed the rest of mankind how great a child of God can be – but in heaven, they are expected to repeat one simple-minded task again and again and again. Why would God go through the trouble of creating a Picasso just to take away his paintbrush?

And it's not just the greats – it's all of us. We all went through weird adventures, we all faced difficult moral dilemmas, hardship and tragedy, we all did our best to contribute to a family or to the world; we built a personality, a life, a little universe within each of us; we took our time on earth and made of it a unique story, a living artwork.

Yet, none of that appears to impress God, our Creator, in the least. In fact, God seems so unimpressed with his creations that he plans to completely erase everything we've become.

Granted, in the traditional version of eternity we would at least be happy. But it's a mindless kind of happiness, like a dog is happy at the foot of his master. The dog doesn't mind eating the same food every day, going for the same walk every day, facing no real challenges, never changing. It's as if God put in a lot of effort creating man, then realized what he really wanted was several billion pets.

To Mormons, earth life is the unique gift of individuality. This is where we develop a conscience and a personality and learn what love is. It is not only a testing ground, it is where we discover who we really are, and it lays the foundation for all the phases of our lives yet to come. The Mormon vision of eternity is a vision of the eternal self. It recognizes the human being as a divine work that each of us helps creates in our lifetime, a thing worth preserving and continuing, a thing God loves so much he cannot let it disappear.

Here on earth I loved movies, having a beer with friends and a woman's laughter. The God of the Mormons says: That's who you are, that's who you will be in the next life. I want to continue having beers with friends and get to know new friends, or whatever the eternal equivalent would be, in the next life. And yes, I have long since figured out that I'm not one of the big winners who get to live in the highest kingdom and create worlds of his own. That's disappointing, but maybe I'm just not that kind of guy. But I am *some* kind of guy. I'm a guy, for example, who likes to observe and learn and experience and think about those things. I want to continue doing that – on another level, perhaps – in the next life. I'm the kind of guy who likes to write his thoughts and dreams down in books, and that, too, I want to keep doing. And if life in eternity should throw me a challenge I'm not prepared for and if I run into trouble and change, all the better. I want to continue being the unique creation that God and I have made during my time here on earth.

In the endlessness that is eternity, traditional Christians are meant to be able to look back on earth life and say, "I'm glad that's over." Mormons will look back and say: "You know, it was tough, but sometimes I think those were the best years of our lives."

CHAPTER 4

Leaving the Garden

THE TALK CAME UNEXPECTED AND ALL AT ONCE.

It was on a Sunday. A. and I sat on an iron bench against the orange-tiled wall in the underground Munich subway station Marienplatz, waiting for our train. We had just come from church and were heading home, dressed in Sunday clothes – suit and tie for me, a formal dress for her.

I remember a girl. A young girl, dressed in a miniskirt, sexy and flirty and proud of her legs, walk past. My eyes followed her, and immediately a voice inside me jumped in and gave me a good talking-to: *Get your eyes off her legs, you're lusting after her, that's your animal side taking over, control yourself, you're dirty.*

Then, strangely, and for the first time in my life, another voice spoke back:

Why not? She's a beautiful girl with beautiful legs, which, by the way, she is presenting to the world to be admired. How does that make me dirty? Wasn't it God himself who gave men the desire for women? Am I making the world a worse place by watching a pretty girl walk by? Why must I feel bad every time I see a pretty girl walking down the street? Is this really why God put men and women on earth, so they can flagellate themselves whenever they catch a glimpse of pretty legs? I've spent so much of my life feeling horrible about myself, how much longer do I have to continue doing that before God is happy with me?

I watched her until she was out of sight.

It was a fight. I forced myself to keep my eyes on her. Then I turned to A. and told her I would no longer be going to church on Sundays.

She had seen it coming. She even understood implications I didn't see. A look of deep despair crept over her and she said, "Then it's over between us, too."

That was shocking. Why would she jump to that conclusion? I tried to convince her. "It's just about the church," I said, "I just have to think things through, I haven't even decided to leave the church, really, but even then, that doesn't mean it's over between us. I still love you."

I told her that, and it was true: "I still love you."

It didn't impress her. She knew something I didn't: Love is not enough.

People like to say that love conquers all – you hear it constantly in pop songs and the movies – but it's not true. A relationship needs a foundation, something you have in common beyond emotion that makes the relationship a significant part of your lives. Without that foundation, love is an emotional hobby. For us, that foundation was our devotion to God, it was the memory of that intense spiritual moment when we both descended into the water of the baptismal font and I raised my right hand and used the priesthood invested in my by God to conclude a covenant between her and our Creator.

After my mission, I had returned to Hawaii, where we stayed in contact by letters and very expensive phone calls. Getting back together with half the world between us became a project. I worked as many jobs as I could and didn't spend a cent. I researched life in Germany as an American ex-pat and found out that I could probably get a work permit as an English-language teacher. In preparation, I studied linguistics and Teaching

English as a Second Language for two years at the Brigham Young University (Hawaii) and the University of Hawaii.

Then I returned to Krefeld and married her.

I was 23, she had just turned 18. She had to get permission from her teachers to take the day off school to get married, and her friends cut class to come along. Then we got in a car and drove down to Switzerland and got sealed to each other for time and all eternity in the temple there.

Now, sitting in a subway station in Munich, she knew: Once the church was gone, our love would follow. I didn't, but she did.

A year or two later, one rainy night following a long session of screaming and tears (my efforts to "find myself" had predictably led me to find myself in bed with another woman), she asked me to leave our apartment, and I did.

That night, so quickly after my faith had died, love died too.

Even today, I want to believe there is a God, but I can't. I can never again believe in the Mormon church, nor in any other church.

I can't put my finger on the exact moment I no longer believed. I can only count off the moments that led to my loss of faith.

The first came in Krefeld. It was the day I walked out of a man's apartment into the sunlight and saw the asphalt of a near-empty parking lot dissolve into a vast bottomless black pit – the day I first realized that if there is no God, there is nothing.

From that point onward, I looked at my church differently.

The first major opportunity to see things I might not have noticed otherwise came as I was leaving Germany at the close of my mission.

That morning I had told the woman who was to become my wife that I had feelings for her, then I got on the train. By evening I was sitting in the living room of a large house in Frankfurt with about a dozen other young men and women who had just served their God for two years and now were pumped up about heading home and rediscovering the world of friends and family, future plans, parties and girls.

It was a strange mood. *Trunky* we called it – because our trunks were packed: nervous and light-headed, but also aware of a certain desperation deep in our hearts. We were at once antsy to get home (at least once a day for the last two years we'd pondered the central question, "What's the first thing you're going to do when you get back?"), proud for sticking it out (having gone through it, we now knew what an achievement it was just to keep going) and sad for leaving people and a place most of us had fallen in love with.

Before we retired to the dining room to eat a final meal together, our mission president called us into his office one by one for our final interviews – a kind of mission debriefing. I sat across from his desk and he peppered me with well-meaning and slightly disinterested questions: How did I feel about my mission? What was I planning to do when I got home? He congratulated me on a job well done and told me how much the church appreciated my work and that he had personally enjoyed watching me grow as I tackled the challenges before me. He warned me about the girls – Mormon girls compete hotly for "RMs," or returned missionaries, as they are considered especially excellent marriage material – and that I should not marry the first one who made eyes at me just because I had been starved for so long.

Then he asked me to sign a sheet of paper.

I took a look at it. It was a personal contract between him and me.

In it, I was to promise never to do certain things: I would never drink alcohol, engage in premarital sex, I would marry a Mormon and always remain faithful to the church.

What was he asking of me? A contract? With him? Why with him?

A mission president, like everyone else in the church, is just a regular guy who is called to lead and manage a few hundred missionaries in a faraway place on his own dime. Mission presidents tend to be older men who were successful back home, usually in business. After all, he has to be able to afford to leave home and work for three years. Plus, if you want to manage a horde of homesick, hormone-ridden young men and women in a foreign country, having once operated a company goes a long way.

But that's all they are. When he got home from his mission, he would just be some guy living in retirement in Idaho or Montana tending his garden and making sandwiches for lunch. Like everyone else.

Mormons do not make covenants with men. They make covenants with God. The covenant I made was my baptism, and I renewed it and deepened it in the temple. It was a covenant between God and a child of God.

That sheet of paper was a contract between me and some guy. He wasn't just asking me to make the same commitments to him I had already made to God, he was asking me to go further: It stipulated that I would check in with him regularly to confirm I was keeping our contract. It even made me promise not to grow my hair long.

Did he think a covenant with him – with some guy – was stronger, more valid, more persuasive than a covenant with God? Would I think twice about breaking a covenant with him, but would break my covenant with God with a mere shrug? Or had he simply acquired a taste for wielding an outsized moral authority over a gang of young men and wanted to hang onto that feeling for as long as he could?

Suddenly it was there again, the black pit: If the church was fake, death was absolute.

"I can't sign this," I said.

"Why not?" he asked.

"Because I already made these promises to God." I didn't mention that I had definitely decided to grow my hair long.

"But this is more immediate because you know me, I'm here, we can talk."

I told him that no contract with a man could replace, supplement or improve upon a covenant with God.

He smiled, nodded and said, "That's fine."

And that was that. I shook his hand and headed back out the door.

Stepping into the living room where the others were still standing around, I felt a wave of relief and gratitude flood over me. It was a test – to see if I was mature enough to understand the covenants I had entered into, and to differentiate between blind obedience and mature, independent decision-making. I felt redeemed. A test! And I had passed! As I entered into the next phase of my life, the man who had watched over me for two years had taught me yet another valuable lesson. I was grateful.

One of my former companions was there. I forget his name now, but we had served together for a few months in – if my memory serves me well – Wuppertal. I walked over to him and asked, "So, what did you do about the contract?"

He shrugged. "I signed it," he said.

There it was again – the black pit. It opened up right in front of me, in my mission president's living room. It was no test. He had tried to extend the moral authority he had over me from my mission into ... well, into the rest of my life. He had tried to replace God.

I never told anyone about it. I still don't know whether it was just his stupid idea or if all mission presidents did the same. I didn't care.

When I got home, I reported to the congregation about how my mission went and bore my testimony and flirted with the girls and told my parents all about my adventures and made plans for the future, but my ears were perked now. Again and again I would hear little echoes of my mission president's power grab and I would wonder: How much of this church is about bringing us to God, how much is about playing God?

All churches are about power to some extent, and that's not always a bad thing. A church is a collection of people with the shared goal of returning to God, and the role of the church is to help us. Just as we give the state the responsibility of telling us when we can and cannot cross the street or drive a car or fire a gun, we invest the church with the power to admonish us to do what is right. Critics of religion call it "indoctrination," but you can also think of it less melodramatically as "teaching," "exhortation," even "social control," or simply "our common goal of returning to God" – that's how I think of it, because I participated in it willingly and I profited from it. But at some point, "teaching" becomes "manipulation," and that is when the church ceases to serve the member, but instead the member becomes a servant to the church.

I thought I saw that turning point when I got back to Hawaii.

While I was away, a new phrase had crept into Mormon society I hadn't noticed before: "The greatest commandment is obedience to the church."

Before I left for my mission, the highest commandment had been, "Thou shalt love the Lord thy God with all thy heart," as Jesus had made clear, and the second greatest was, "Thou shalt love thy neighbor as thyself" (Matthew 22:35–40).

Suddenly, it was "obedience to the church," even "to church leaders."

When I put my objections to my priesthood leaders, I got an elegantly Orwellian answer: "Sure, to love God and one another are the highest commandments, but by their very nature as commandments, you have to obey them, and since God speaks to us through the church, the law of obedience to the church is higher."

I even understood the reasons for this change.

The hippie revolution of the seventies had mutated into the so-called "culture wars" that are still plaguing the nation today, and the conservative values of the Eisenhower Era were taking heavy damage. Everyone in a position of responsibility in the church was scared to death that young Mormons would be lost to rampant hedonism (thus my mission president's worries about hair length). The reaction was to tighten the leash: Though we were theoretically taught that we were sent to earth to learn how to use our free will, in practical terms we were expected to trade in our free will for obedience to the will of the church. But for me, now, the church was just doing the same thing my mission president had tried to do: Replace a covenant between man and God with a covenant between man and man.

The more I thought about it, the more I wondered if even my baptism had been a true covenant with God – or if it was just a covenant with men.

After that, everywhere I looked, I saw a church built on power and manipulation.

Starting with sex.

On the surface, the church has an almost liberal attitude toward sex, at least compared to some conservative churches. While Catholicism, for example, officially teaches that sex is for reproduction only and disapproves of birth control, Mormonism teaches that God gave us sex for pleasure as well.

But there's a caveat. While sex within marriage is okay, all other kinds are of the Devil. And there are so many dangerous types that acceptable sex becomes the exception:

Sex before marriage leads to unwanted pregnancy (and puts you in Satan's hands); adultery leads to divorce and revoked temple privileges (and puts you in Satan's hands); sexual experimentation, even in marriage, will lead to sexual addiction and to wanting ever more and ever stranger sex, until you are a pervert who can't get enough (and end up in Satan's hands).

It's like reassuring a man who's afraid of flying that the statistical chances of an airplane crashing are virtually nil, then subjecting him to hours of video footage of planes going up in flames. The sheer volume of warnings about sex loads the concept down with so much guilt and fear that even in marriage with a loving partner, you can't help but feel you're doing something despicable.

Teenagers get the full brunt of it.

Church leaders have at their disposal a wide range of parables and metaphors, myths and aphorisms designed to make kids associate sex with horrible feelings about themselves. (And it's not just Mormons – when I talk to friends from other Protestant denominations, they recognize the same stories and likenesses. I'm surprised no literary scholar out there has ever come up with the idea of writing an "Encyclopedia of Scaring Kids Off Sex.")

Girls are taught that if they have sex before marriage, they will be defiled and no good man will want to marry them: "Don't be a doorknob everyone gets to turn," "Marrying a girl who has already given herself to someone else is like eating the cupcake after someone has licked it." Young girls' bodies are routinely compared to worn tennis shoes, used cars and chewed gum. And of course, if you engage in premarital sex, you can't get married in the temple – you have to marry outside, and then everyone knows you're a slut.

Boys are told, "If it scratches, don't itch." They are taught to take a cold shower when evil thoughts come upon them, and it's implied that females only submit to sex to please the male, but really suffer during it, which makes any kind of sex a form of rape in the mind of the Mormon man. Even when I was married, I felt guilty and selfish suggesting to my wife that we fool around a little.

Again and again, teenagers are taught that the body is a holy temple – once you defile the temple with sex, the Holy Spirit cannot dwell there. (Only much later did I wonder how sex can defile a holy temple while junk food, air pollution, genetic defects and cancer can't.)

Growing up a Mormon, I expended endless amounts of energy trying not to think about sex. I failed, of course. You can't beat hormones. What I ended up with was not a pristine temple, but with an impenetrable black cloud of guilt and self-loathing that infested my soul for years – and to some extent still does.

Of course, that's the whole point: You're supposed to feel guilty. Guilt is a tool to make you dependent.

And don't pretend to be shocked. All religions use sex and guilt feelings about sex to bind members to the institution. Even Buddha, in his very first official discourse, the *Dhammacakkappavattana Sutta*, made clear that sex is one of the "cravings" that causes suffering and needs to be overcome. It's like a drug: Guilt gets you addicted, and the church is the dealer. Think of a kid growing up – he can't stop himself from masturbating, much less protect himself from "evil thoughts." That's biologically not possible. So if you can find a way to make that kid feel awful about himself every time he sees a pair of pretty legs walk by, he will need to go to church again and again to absolve himself of his self-loathing. The guiltier you feel, the more you need the church to relieve your guilt.

At the start of this book I discussed the Book of Mormon verse I love most and promised to discuss the one I hate most. This is it:

"Natural man is an enemy to God." (Mosiah 3:19)

It's a sentence that embodies not only Mormonism but all of Protestant Christianity. Especially Calvinist Protestantism teaches that the animal side of man – physical desire, from sex to any kind of pleasure – must be repressed. Feel attracted to that girl walking past in a miniskirt? Don't look. Want a drink?

Don't do it – it could lead to horrible things. The sentence, "Natural man is an enemy to God" divides the human soul into two parts – the animal and the divine. Those two sides are enemies. If you want to develop your divine nature, first you must beat back your disgusting animal lusts.

Interestingly enough, it was neither Joseph Smith nor John Calvin who invented the doctrine of repressing desire. Jesus himself taught in the Sermon on the Mount that animal lust should be quashed, even at the price of self-mutilation:

"Ye have heard that it was said by them of old time, Thou shalt not commit adultery: But I say unto you, That whosoever looketh on a woman to lust after her hath committed adultery with her already in his heart. And if thy right eye offend thee, pluck it out, and cast it from thee: for it is profitable for thee that one of thy members should perish, and not that thy whole body should be cast into hell." (Matthew 5:27–29)

Jesus goes further even than the Mormons: God doesn't only expect man to repress his physical desires – he expects him to be without sin in every way. Jesus closes the Sermon on the Mount with these words:

"Be ye therefore perfect, even as your Father which is in heaven is perfect." (Matthew 5:48)

This sentence, too, is a favorite of Mormons. Only when I was older did I understand why it was repeated endlessly: It demands of human beings what we cannot give, and by doing so ties us even closer to the church. The sentence puts mankind on a moral treadmill and makes him strive eternally for something that is not there. No matter what some spaced-out hermit in the desert may claim, it is not possible for a human being to be "perfect." The church pretends to support us in our striving for moral perfection, but in truth it sends us over a cliff flapping our arms, for all we accomplish is to dangle our own moral inadequacy before our eyes all day long.

Even prayer – the most intimate facet of Mormon spirituality – can make a church member more dependent.

Mormons are proud of their concept of prayer. They do not memorize prayers, they do not see prayers as a liturgy – for a Mormon, prayer is speaking with God, and we expect God to hold up his part of the conversation. We can ask God for anything. For guidance, for comfort, for help making important decisions or getting through a crisis.

Soon you get into the habit of praying at every major juncture, and the deeper you get into Mormonism, the more you pray, until at some point it takes over. Soon you aren't just praying for guidance in a major decision, you are praying for guidance in every little thing.

What about buying a new car? You like the green one, but you like the blue one too. If you pray for guidance in everything, at some point you will find yourself on your knees asking for guidance in choosing the color. It makes sense: What if you happen to be parked somewhere and a guy walks by and says, "Hey, green is my favorite color, too," and you get into a conversation and find out that he is seeking the meaning of life, and you invite him to come to church next Sunday and he comes and is converted and his soul is saved. You think back and say: "Wow, that's why God wanted me to buy the green car." But what if you didn't pray and instead bought the blue car? The guy will walk right by and end up in hell.

I'm exaggerating a little. In the end, how much a Mormon prays, and for what, depends on his/her personality and the circumstances. If you are really in love with the green car, you don't pray about it, just as I never prayed about whether I should try to become a writer, or move to Europe, or get married – I wanted to do it, so I did it.

Having said that, I have often had "green car" discussions with other members about their struggle to find guidance in the smallest, most ridiculous things.

At some point, I found myself praying about everything.

Prayer for guidance in all things goes hand in hand with a deep conviction that everything is either right or wrong. Just as drinking alcohol was wrong, buying the blue car could be wrong. Mormons want to live right – so I was always trying to figure out what was right, often in matters of very little importance. Without noticing it, I became dependent on a higher authority for nearly every decision I made. I didn't trust myself to make the right decision alone. I couldn't believe that sometimes there is no right or wrong, that it's just a choice. I had to get it right, I had to ask. It didn't occur to me that this was the behavior of a child, always looking to mother or father for approval. But it wasn't Mom and Dad I was dependent on, it was God – and his representative here on earth, the church.

Looking back, it angers me and grieves me in equal parts: Prayer was such a comfort to me, such a privilege – the right to speak with the Creator! And at the same time, it was a tool to keep me dependent.

In the end, I could have lived with a lot of things – the contradictions, the doubts, all that. If you believe, you can live with a lot. If you have faith, you are willing to suffer for it.

What I couldn't live with was the self-loathing.

The moment my love of God turned to self-loathing came one Sunday in church in Munich when I was just shy of thirty.

I remember sitting near the back, with my wife, listening to another member speak from the pulpit. The pews were sparsely populated, people listened politely or paged through hymnals or the scriptures or something else. A few rows in front of me, a couple of children had their heads down over something that was more interesting – a coloring book, maybe.

Suddenly I realized how often I had heard everything the brother was saying from the pulpit. Every word I had heard before: the parables, the personal anecdote, the testimony of faith, the admonition to keep the commandments, the little joke, the homey metaphor about the dog that trusts its master unquestioningly and the responsibility that brings. Not only that, I realized that it would be like this forever – every Sunday, I would be sitting here listening to things I had heard a thousand times before, over and over again, until the day I died.

Outside the church walls, life was happening.

It was the late eighties. The Cold War was still on, atomic bombs were piling up, the Middle East was a mess, politicians seemed to be irresponsible lunatics, there was terrorism everywhere, society was tearing itself to pieces. It was a big, frightening, confusing world.

And here in church...what was the issue of the day?

Coca-Cola.

Likes all new ideas, the Word of Wisdom, as brilliant as it was, also brought new problems. The Mormon health code forbade "hot drinks," a 19th-century term generally interpreted to mean coffee and black tea. Mormons further interpret God's dislike for "hot drinks" as related to the fact that they contain caffeine. Caffeine is, after all, a drug.

Coca-Cola was not a "hot drink," but it did contain caffeine. Complicating things was the fact that it was invented after the Word of Wisdom. Thus, Mormons today are faced with a dilemma: Does God want us to retroactively interpret the Word of Wisdom to include Coke, or would he come out and say it explicitly – in a new revelation – if he didn't want us to drink it? Church authorities, when asked about the issue, say that it's up to the individual. Ah, but they forget that telling Mormons that something is entirely up to them is like asking a cat to decide whether it wants to be inside or outside.

There are two factions: The Coke-drinking faction appears weak and hedonistic, as if they were flirting with sin; the Coke-abstaining faction has the "better safe than sorry" principle on its side, but it also gets a little too much satisfaction out of implying that they are somehow following a "higher law" that inferior Mormons aren't quite ready for.

Outside: real life. Inside: the Coke dilemma.

I had to get out. I had to stand up and walk out. I knew this was not what God put us on earth to do. I knew I could not live my own life if I sat there a minute longer.

But I couldn't.

There is always a right and wrong, you see, and not attending church – much less leaving in the middle of services – was wrong. I had been raised – I had made it my declared goal in life – to do the right thing. Now I saw I had reached that goal: I had become a good Mormon, as witnessed by the fact that I couldn't bring myself to perform the simple emancipatory act of walking out of a church meeting, even though I knew I was wasting my time.

As I sat there grinding my teeth, tense and desperate, fighting with myself, I reexamined my life.

I did not see a grown man.

I had left Hawaii and come to Germany not only to marry and study the Middle Ages, but also to get away from my overbearing family and gain a taste of independence. To be the captain of my own fate, to live my own life. To grow up.

But I had taken the church with me. The church told me exactly how to behave, just as my mother and father told me when I was a child. I looked at myself and I saw a thirteen-year-old, looking to the church in lieu of Mom and Dad for authority. I was nearly thirty, yet I was still incapable of taking command of my own life.

I sat there, unable to move, and hated myself. The shame and self-loathing grew once church was over and I was outside, walking to the subway with my wife. Then, in the subway, waiting for the train, watching a pretty girl walk by, I turned to A. and told her that I would not be going back to church next Sunday and not for a long time after that, either.

My favorite Mormon fable to scare kids away from sin is the one about the frog in the pot (it's one of those parables that many Protestant churches use). It goes something like this:

If you throw a frog into a pot of water boiling on the stove, it will immediately jump out to save its life. But if you throw a frog into a pot of cold water and slowly turn up the heat until it reaches a boil, the frog won't notice the gradual increase and will sit there, content, until it is boiled to death.

It's a parable about sin: You might start out with a small sin, something innocuous, something even God can't really get upset about, but once that sin feels normal, you go on to the next sin, and the next, and before you know it, you are lying in a gutter dressed in a leather bondage outfit with a needle sticking out of your arm.

That's the problem Mormons really have with Coke: It's the gateway drug to alcohol.

That week, I went out and bought a Coke and drank it for the first time. It didn't taste like sin – it tasted like a sugary drink.

A week or so later – with our Sundays free, we had a little more time on our hands – we were walking through a Christmas market that had just opened on Marienplatz in downtown Munich. We pushed our way through the tightly packed crowds in their winter clothes and splurged on a bratwurst and a sack of roasted chestnuts. Then we found ourselves before a stand that offered *Glühwein*, a hot, spicy Christmas punch laced with wine.

I had grown up in a household without alcohol. For me, alcohol was all about sin, crime and danger. I had never been in a bar – even walking past one of those dark and cave-like dens of sin made me shudder. If I knew someone who drank, though I never said anything, in my mind he was one step away from being a criminal, and the sight of a wine bottle in a friend's kitchen lent the entire household a hint of unrepentant decadence. Yes, I was afraid of alcohol – as I was raised to be.

But now I was ashamed of constantly being afraid – afraid of alcohol, afraid of people with a different lifestyle, afraid of the world outside the boundaries of God's commandments, afraid of the risks of life, afraid of life itself. I was sick and tired of being the frog in the pot, I wanted to be a human being in charge of his own life.

My wife was different. As long as she was in the church and believed, she followed the commandments, but she had grown up with alcohol in the house and was not afraid of it. She knew what I was thinking and said, "If you're going to do this, you have to go all the way."

I told her, "If I start acting weird, if I take my clothes off and run around naked and try to dance on a table or anything like that, stop me, okay?"

She promised she would. Then I drank the punch.

Nothing happened.

No, that's not entirely true. Something did happen. I looked around.

Marienplatz was full of parents with their children, boys and girls on dates, normal people buying trinkets, chatting, laughing, arguing, standing in line, taking photos of each other. No one was dancing naked on a table, no one was taking out a knife to settle a disagreement, no one was rolling around in a gutter. They were all normal people. Just normal people.

I wondered then how much of life I had missed. How much life had passed me by while I was huddled together with a lot of other Mormons discussing how best to remain uncontaminated, uncompromised, not endangered by the big bad world out there.

This was God's creation. This sprawling churning carnival of sheer unpredictable human life. I recalled my favorite Book of Mormon passage: "There needs be opposition in all things."

So all of this – the Mormons and the non-Mormons, the Coke-drinkers and the non-Coke-drinkers, the good and the bad and the right and the wrong and all those people in between – all of this was what God made.

All of a sudden I could no longer imagine a God sternly judging us for our evil thoughts. I could not imagine a God demanding that human life conform to a single set of principles valid for all. I could not even imagine a God that would demand his children sit in church every Sunday for hours on end sweating in their Sunday clothes and listening to some guy telling them what is wrong with them and every day worrying about whether they had looked too long at a pretty girl or if they were going to be punished for that one time they drank a little Coke when they were teenagers. I could no longer imagine a God looking down on a lot of families wandering through the Christmas market chatting, spending money, joking, maybe getting a little tipsy, enjoying their day with each other, judging them and taking down their names for later punishment.

In the months that followed, I did a lot of thinking about Adam and Eve.

The Mormons teach the story of the Garden of Eden very unlike any other church. There is no "Original Sin." Eve was not the first sinner, she was the smart one. Satan – in the form of the serpent – was just doing what God told him to. And most importantly: By reluctantly eating the apple, Adam solved an unsolvable paradox.

I remember a missionary companion of mine in Dortmund, I think it was. (He was an interesting guy – I realize now he was probably a kleptomaniac. We would walk out of a department store and he would open his satchel to look for the bus plan and I would see new bicycle tube patches or a pack of Bic pens, and I would say, "Hey, we didn't buy anything, what's that?" and he would say, "Oh, it must have fallen in while I was walking past the display." Smart guy, though.) Once, he said something out of the blue that I will never forget: "In paradox there is truth."

It was a startling thing to say. It has stuck with me ever since. I think about it when I recall Nephi's words about opposition in all things – no good without evil, no happiness without grief, you have to be cruel to be kind.

Paradox is the key to the Mormon version of the story of Adam and Eve.

When God placed Adam and Eve in the Garden, he gave them two contradicting commandments.

The first was "to multiply and replenish the earth" – in other words, to have sex. Alas, as described in the Bible, Adam and Eve were "innocent" – they did not know what sex was, they didn't even understand that they were naked. They were prepubescent children in adult bodies.

There was a solution, of course: In the Garden grew the Tree of Knowledge of Good and Evil. One bite of the fruit of this tree would give them the necessary boost into maturity.

Unfortunately, God's second commandment was: Never eat of the fruit of the Tree of Knowledge of Good and Evil. God made it very clear there would be dire consequences if Adam or Eve ate of that fruit: They would be cast out of the Garden, out of the presence of God, and in the world outside they would find hardship, suffering, confusion and death.

The paradox, then, is this: No matter which commandment they followed, they would be breaking the other. In Mormon cosmology, paradox is a real part of life.

Church authorities would never say it in those terms, but if you pay attention in the temple, the story of Adam and Eve teaches us that obedience to God can only be fulfilled by disobedience.

No one knows how long Adam and Eve wandered innocently about the Garden of Eden, from tree to bush to grassy riverside. I imagine it was long enough for them to get bored. At some point, it became apparent they had no intention whatsoever of touching that fruit. So God turned to Plan B: He sent Lucifer to the Garden. That's right: The Devil's presence in the Garden of Eden was God's doing. And that's a good thing. If Lucifer hadn't shown up, Adam and Eve would still be wandering around the Garden today, petting lions, picking flowers and living off nuts and berries.

It tells you something about how Joseph Smith saw women that in his version Eve knew what she was doing when she bit into the apple – she was smart enough to comprehend the hidden message behind the paradox. And her motives were also typically Mormon: family. She understood that the family she was sent here to create – the human race – was impossible without disobeying God and facing death outside the Garden, outside God's presence. In Mormonism, Eve's act of disobedience is a declaration of independence from God.

The Mormon Garden of Eden is a parable of living: You grow up innocent and protected, your parents take care of everything and teach you a simplified version of life: Do what Mom and Dad tell you, never lie, clean up your room and eat your vegetables, be obedient and everything will be okay. That's legitimate from Mom and Dad's perspective. They see you as a child and want to protect you from the dangers of the adult world. To their minds, the worst thing you can do is disobey – that puts you at risk. Stay safe. Stay at home. Follow the rules. As long as you remain in the Garden, Mom and Dad can protect you.

Then comes puberty. You become aware of sex and with sex comes the need for independence. You start doing things Mom and Dad don't want you to do, and eventually you eat the fruit of the Tree of Knowledge of Good and Evil and you get kicked out of the Garden.

Life out here in the real world isn't as fun as you thought it would be.

Back in the security of home, you used to rail against the hypocrisy of the adult world; now you need the money to pay the rent, so you suck up to a boss you hate. You used to have a vision of peace and harmony; now you realize that other people aren't going to treat you as fairly as Mom and Dad did, and that a lot of the rules they taught you at home don't apply here. You have to decide what kind of person you want to be. Much of the time you don't live up to your own standards.

But that's the whole point. Life at home, life in the Garden, life with God in the pre-existence was one-dimensional. Only on the outside can you grow into who you really are.

Even today my thoughts keep returning to this *ur*-parable of life – the story of the Garden of Eden. And always I arrive at the same conclusion:

If there is a God, we are not supposed to know that.

The moment he communicates with us – via prophets, belief systems or wise books – he negates the principle that we have to find our path independently. To ensure our independence, God cannot tell us the truth about himself. His greatest gift to us is closing the door, turning his back and walking away. Any religion, including Christianity, any holy book, including the Bible, any prophet, including Joseph Smith, even Jesus, may well be valuable, but were not sent from God. The story of the Garden of Eden stands at the beginning of the Bible like a divine disclaimer, telling us that the wisdom and truths to follow were not written by God – which, ironically, includes the story of the Garden of Eden itself.

This, then, was my personal paradox: The church had taught me my purpose here on earth, but to fulfill that purpose, I had to leave the church. If I wanted to obey God, I had to disobey him. If I believed in God, I had to stop believing in him.

When, at some point not long after I turned thirty, I was living alone in a small student apartment behind the University in Munich. I had finally received my Master's in Medieval German

Literature, but besides that I had only debts and no profession. For a few years now I had not attended church, instead I thought endlessly about the Garden of Eden, about the God I had loved, and about how I was going to manage life outside the church.

Again and again I kept putting off taking the last step. But I knew I owed it to myself and to God. So one night I knelt down in my little room above a bar and prayed.

I told God I no longer knew whether he existed or not. I hoped he did exist, but I was no longer certain. I told him that – in case he did – I owed him an explanation. That's why I was kneeling here. The God who had accompanied me all my life, the God with whom I had closed a covenant, had the right to know why I was turning from him.

I said that I had never grown up, that I was still living like a child, that the church and God himself were a kind of substitute parents whom I gave too much responsibility for my life. I said I wasn't behaving the way I expected of myself. I said I wanted to live like a grown man in my own eyes. I wanted to face life with all its risks and dangers, without hiding behind God. I wanted to make mistakes and to admit to them and if I failed, then it would be my failure.

I said I was leaving him now. I would no longer be attending church, I would no longer be keeping his commandments, and I would no longer pray to him.

I did not ask for forgiveness. I did not ask for understanding or for permission, nor did I ask for his help in my further life, though I was sorely tempted. I simply said goodbye. I closed my prayer as all Mormons close their prayers, in the name of his son, Jesus Christ, and with "Amen."

Then I stood up and went about the business of becoming myself.

When you tell someone you left a religion like Mormonism, they expect to hear about your liberation and how grateful you are finally to be able to lead a normal life.

What they don't understand is that when you push religion out of your life, you let death in, like an unwanted guest you can't get rid of. The moment I left, the black pit opened up below me and will never close again.

People smirk when I say this. It's fashionable today to pretend to stand above the fear of death, as if fear were for lesser beings. It's hip to say: "When you die, your molecules join with other molecules out there and you'll be part of the sun and stars, part of the flowers and the ocean and the trees. Isn't that a wonderful idea?"

No, it's not a wonderful idea. It's a kitschy idea. You can tell it's kitschy because it falls apart the moment you reformulate it: "As a molecule, you'll become one with dog shit, exhaust fumes and excess belly fat."

Molecules are not conscious. They do not have personalities. They do not think or feel. Going from a self-reflective human being to a collection of molecules is simply going from something to nothing. That's all dying is. There is nothing exciting or romantic about it when everything you were in this life, all the love and hope and suffering and experience, is suddenly erased as if it were never there.

The dream of spending eternity with God is the only acceptable antidote to death, and the Mormon vision of eternity is the most beautiful dream there is.

I just don't dream it anymore.

So what remains, now that God is over?

I feel free.

I'm a little surprised today at how fast I was able to distance myself from certain Mormon beliefs. Whenever I meet up with

Mormon friends, I see the old fears once more, like the fear of sex – premarital sex, "evil thoughts," sex scenes in movies – but now fear of sex feels unreal, like some bizarre psychological experiment in which people were raised from childhood isolated in a tiny room somewhere far from reality and only fed distorted information about the world outside.

Since leaving, life has become broader, airier, more interesting. Mormons have their own culture and tend to make it the center of their lives. That makes sense: They need each other's help avoiding the temptations of the world. But the air in there can get stifling, and the horizon is too close. Even if you have friends on the outside, as a Mormon you eat, think, talk and dream Mormonism, and it can get old. My friends on the outside are not better people or more intelligent or better informed (on the contrary – if you're looking for "good" people, people who are more honest and sincere, friendlier, more reliable, less hypocritical than the average, check out the Mormons), but they have a wider variety of experiences and interests, their taboos and fears are fewer.

And it's not just the people: Life on the outside is more interesting in general. To put it in religious terms (and I still think in religious terms), as a Mormon, my view of God's creation resembled one of those covers of a Jehovah's Witnesses brochure: The lamb lying down with the lion, Eden-like harmony, peace and love and a healthy measure of conformity.

Now I see the world more like one of those paintings by Hieronymus Bosch, full of crazy, bizarre, shocking mysteries. You might think Hieronymus Bosch was painting nightmares, but I see a world full of fantastic, unexpected wonders, boundless in its variety, and I am in love with the sheer weirdness of it all.

At the same time, people on the outside can be just as dogmatic, judgmental and shortsighted as on the inside. Nowadays I notice it most when it comes to politics.

I was raised socially and politically conservative and have since drifted somewhat toward the left, so I know both sides of the spectrum. As a rule I have experienced conservatives as intelligent, upright, open and deeply humane people. There are exceptions, of course: In the seventies, with all the hippies and hedonism going around, many conservatives thought of liberals as fools of Satan bent on destroying the world, and that hysteria is still there today. Liberals, on the other hand, seemed more willing to hear both sides of the story – they appeared more intellectual to me and thus more attractive.

Today, both sides are steeped in the same hysteria, convinced of rigid, unrealistic, caricature-like ideas of the other side. On the left, that is especially visible in the various lines of thought we label "political correctness," much of which has mutated into hateful ideologies that serve only to vilify and dehumanize people who come from another culture of belief.

I thought I was done with ideologies behind when I left Mormonism, but they thrive where you least expect them. It's as if there were some primal human need to raise yourself above others, and if you can't do it by carrying the bigger gun or driving the bigger car, you do it by subscribing to some idea that makes you feel superior. And since religions are no longer cool, we replace God and his commandments with some other issue that we inflate into an existential question of life and death. Just like Mormonism turns problems like alcohol or premarital sex into a matter of losing your eternal soul, modern ideologies will blame you for the imminent destruction of society, even of the entire planet, if you eat the wrong foods or make a joke in bad taste.

I'll bet you laughed when I talked about Mormons discussing the Coca-Cola question, but many people outside the church do exactly the same, just with different topics. Whenever I have to sit through another long sermon about gluten intolerance or micro-aggressions or non-verbal racism or whatever, as if it were a matter of life and death, I find myself thinking: "You would make a great Mormon." All you have to do is replace "Eating meat is wrong" with "Drinking alcohol is sinful," and you've got it. Replace "conservatives are idiots bent on destroying the world" with "non-Mormons are sinners who will go to hell" and you'll fit in just fine. The words are different, but the principle remains the same.

Since leaving, my writing, too, has changed.

When I started out writing, my heroes tended to personify good and my villains were caricatures of evil and they were rewarded or punished accordingly. Nowadays, the first thing I want my readers to know about my characters are the parts they would not tell their parents over Thanksgiving dinner. I'm proud to say that it's hard to identify my heroes as particularly heroic.

I still imagine God's eye upon us – but not God the moral judge, rather God the Creator, who has completed his work and is now relaxing on the couch, one hand in a bag of fat-free potato chips, feet up, zapper in hand, watching TV, and there we are, each of us our own drama, our own comedy, our own channel. He's wondering what turn his creation will take this time; what crazy thing people will think up, how they will react to the new situation, what wrong path the whole chaotic mess will hurtle down next. His cosmic TV with billions of channels offers everything from soap opera to horror, from war movie to science fiction and back to schmaltzy love story with a regular dose of heart-wrenching brutality and a touch of deeply disturbing existential philosophy. I suspect he is just as often saddened and frustrated by his Creation as he is happy with us, but always entertained. Sometimes, when he is again reminded how brutal life is and how cruel humans can be, I imagine he wonders whether he has made a horrible mistake. Perhaps he should go back and start all over again. Then one of us does something beautiful and admirable, or bizarre and unexpected, and he chuckles to himself and mutters, "Naw, I'm not changing a thing."

In many ways I am still the Mormon I was raised to be, and I am grateful to have certain Mormon principles in my life.

Nephi's idea about "opposition in all things," for example.

That scripture by Nephi implies that everything on earth, whether we think of it as good or bad, was intended by God. Everything is God's creation, it's all equally divine. Without even one part of it, existence would become meaningless. I often think back to that Sunday I skipped church and drank a plastic cup of mulled wine at the Christmas market in Munich and looked around and saw not a bunch of sinners, but just a lot of children of God trying to live the life God had given them.

The meaning of life for me today is still more or less the same I learned in the temple, at least as I interpret it: to become the independent being that my Creator expects me to be. There is only one difference: Before, I sought my purpose for living in the life to come; now, I seek it in the life I am living now.

There are a lot of people out there, I'm sure, who can live without a declared purpose, but I am not one of them. As I thought about the meaning of life without God, I returned again and again to the parable of the talents: God gives each of us a different sum of talents, then leaves, but he understands those talents as an investment – when he returns, he wants to see that we have turned a profit.

But what are the talents? What is that original investment? What did God give us that we are all meant to multiply?

It can't be a religion, or a guru, or a holy book – all those things vary according to when and where we are born, they are arbitrary. The meaning of life must be the same for all children of God, and as far as I can see, there are only three things he gave everyone one of us:

- A physical body with needs and limits;
- A spirit or mind capable of much more than we imagine,

- A specific situation we are born into – a family, a nation, certain economic, political and social conditions, a geographic and period in history.

That's it. That's what makes up life.

The meaning of life, then, can only be to make something out of those building blocks we were given at the start. Whether there is a God or not, it doesn't really matter: We don't need to be in contact with God to make something out of life.

The meaning of life as I see it, then, is this: To make something out of life that is more in the end than it was in the beginning.

That's something I think I can do.

I miss God terribly.

When life gets rough, when that black pit opens up beneath my feet, I long for a god who can tell me: This life isn't important, it's the next one that you are living for. But that god is no longer there.

But then the phase passes and I catch myself from falling too far, and again I am grateful and proud that I can at least say this about myself: That I have left the comfort and protection of my personal Garden of Eden and made a life for myself on the outside; that I have become, finally, myself.

About the author

THE AMERICAN WRITER ERIC T. HANSEN GREW UP IN Hawaii and lives and works in Berlin. He fell in love with Germany when on a two-year mission for the Mormon church. It was there he lost his faith, but also realized his dream of studying medieval literature and becoming a writer. His books – all in German – include *Die Nibelungenreise* (Driving Through the Dark Ages), *Planet Germany* and *Planet America*, and novels like the thriller *Neuntöter* with his partner Astrid Ule (under the name Ule Hansen).

Visit Eric T. Hansen on Facebook and at www.ethansen.com.

About Hula Ink

THE MICRO-PUBLISHER HULA INK WAS FOUNDED BY Eric T. Hansen to publish books (e-books and in print) that traditional publishers can't touch – because they are too unusual, have a too limited audience or are simply too short. A handful of writers are committed to publishing their most unusual works there, often under pen names, for example Ernie Poodle, Keiki Kailua and John Street.

Visit Hula Ink on Facebook and at www.hulaink.com.

Acknowledgements

MANY THANKS TO ALL THE FRIENDS (IN REAL LIFE and on Facebook) who supported and encouraged me in this project. Especially to Astrid Ule, who took me through the story again and again and also went through the English and German texts repeatedly until everything made sense; to Andreas Rupprecht, who voluntarily took upon himself the great work of creating a beautiful cover; and to John Grantham, who showed me the difference a good layout can make.

Made in the USA
Middletown, DE
02 October 2017